Superior Catholics

By

Georgeann Cheney

&

Theodora Meronek

Savage **PRESS**

Box 115, Superior, WI 54880 (715) 394-9513

First Edition
Printed in 1997

© Copyright 1997
Savage Press
P.O. Box 115
Superior, WI 54880

All rights reserved, including the right to reproduce this book or portions thereof, in any form, without written permission from the publisher.

This is a memoir. All the information and ascertations are strictly the product of each individual writer's memory and not in any way a construction of the authors or the publisher.

ISBN 1-886028-23-0

Library of Congress Catalog Card Number: 96-072270

Printed in the U.S.A.
at
Morris Press
Kearney, NE

Acknowledgments

They're all gone now. All the little schools that once dotted the neighborhoods of Superior — St. Adalbert's, St. Anthony, St. Francis, St. Louis, St. Patrick's, St. Stanislaus, and Claude Allouez— have closed their doors and are remembered only by the many students who attended them. That is why we wrote this book —so that people would not forget that there was once a thriving parochial education system in Superior. We also wrote it because our family has always had so much fun telling "Catholic school stories", that we were sure that there were others out there just like us. We were right. So many people were willing to share their own stories that writing this book was more fun than work. We would also like to give special thanks to Rosemarie Ruthgeerts-Birch for her fantastic photos, Mike Stranko and Annie Snyder who were so helpful to us at the beginning of this project. Their wonderful stories and photographs of St. Adalbert's were such an incentive and inspiration to us. We also thank Lucy Olaf for putting us in touch with all her connections at St. Pat's and St. Stan's. All of you Billings Park people are great! We would like to thank our publisher, Michael Savage, for all of his encouragement and considerable patience. If we could, Mike, we'd make you a "Superior Catholic". We would like to thank all of the people who so generously contributed to this book —allowing us into their homes and into their memories. There would be no book without you.

— **The Authors**

Dedication

This book is dedicated to the memory of our parents Leo T. Meronek & Mae Osman Meronek, Superior Catholics and superior parents. Also to Father Francis Nowak & Father Oswald Gasper, O.F.M. and to all our friends and relatives from St. Adalbert's, Bog Błogosławy.

This is co-author Georgeann Cheney's 2nd grade class at St. Adalbert's School. How many faces can you identify?

Introducing Sr. Mary Agnes

We would like you to meet Sr. Mary Agnes. She is a nice nun with a great sense of humor, but she still wants you to sit up straight and do your best in penmanship. Don't take her too seriously, remember what Sister Says, "Life is too long to be miserable."

Superior Catholics

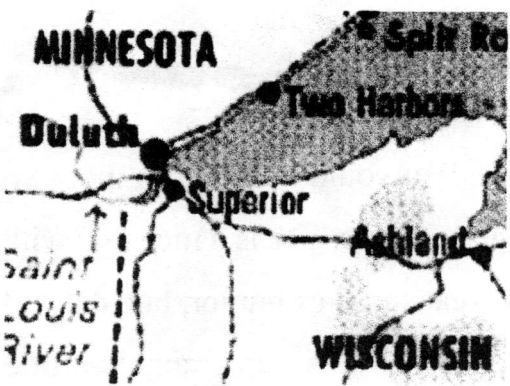

For those of you outside the area who have no idea where Superior is, here's a little map to help.

Superior is a beautiful place to live. The greatest Great Lake and the vast forests surrounding the city makes our home a nearly magical place.

Our winters are dramatic thanks to Lake Superior's effect on the region's climate. Summers are cool in the early going, but fantastic later on. Thanks to the lake's influence, our autumns offer many days of a glorious Indian Summer that makes fall truly wonderful.

Superior is a great place to grow up and, after we're done being the biggest kids around, we know it'll be a great place to mature and become responsible adults (as unlikely as that prospect seems to most of our friends).

Superior is also a great place to visit. Plan a trip, see the sights, go to Mass, eat some pierogi and chat up the locals using "up nort talk."

See ya soon.

— The Polish Sisters

Superior Catholics

Take Your Latin Quiz

At the beginning of each section you'll find a mystery Latin phrase. At least, ever since the Latin Mass was dropped, they're somewhat mysterious. Have fun figuring out what these memorable phrases mean. There may even be one or two that only make sense nonsensically. Go figure!

— The Authors

This is the 1929 championship basketball team from St. Adalbert's. Cool hey?

𝔖uperior 𝔠atholics

About the Cover

The photo on the cover is of our father's graduating class. His name is Mr. Leo Meronek and he is located in the top row in the center. He graduated from St. Adalbert's School.

— The Authors

This is a photo of the interior of St. Adalbert's church.

Table of Contents

St. Adalbert's School.................................. 11

Sts. Anthony and Margaret School............ 43

Cathedral School.. 59

Claude Allouez Academy.......................... 71

St. Francis Xavier School.......................... 77

St. Louis School... 89

St. Patrick's School.................................... 97

St. Stanislaus School................................ 113

Superior Catholic Wanna-bes.................. 121

Spot the Nun Page................................... 138

Superior's Catholic future....................... 139

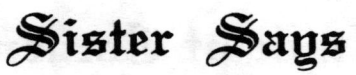

St. Adalbert's

Dominus vobiscum

This photo is of the author's aunts, Sophie and Annie Meronek with their graduating class from St. Adalbert's School. They are in the middle row on the far right.

Superior Catholics

ST. ADALBERT'S
Skoł a Wojciecha'

"Instructions will not be given exclusively in the Polish language," so said Father Anthony Jazdzewski when ground was broken at the corner of Thompson Avenue and East Third Street for the new St. Adalbert's Polish Catholic School. Father Jazdzewski assured everyone that English and other languages would be used to educate the children of the Polish immigrants who made up St. Adalbert's parish, but that their native tongue would predominate.

St. Adalbert's Catholic Church had been organized in 1909 to serve the religious needs of the ever-growing Polish population of the eastern neighborhoods of Superior. A dedication ceremony was held on August 14, 1909 to celebrate the opening of the new church. The ceremonies were preceded by a parade which formed at the corner of East Fifth Street and R Avenue and marched to St. Adalbert's. Martin Talviski, grand marshal, lead the procession which included the Great Northern Band, several Polish societies such as the Polaski Guard and the Catholic Order of Foresters, the clergy riding in coaches, and the Marine Band. Upon arriving at the church, dedication ceremonies, which included a Pontifical High Mass and special blessings from the Pope at Rome, were held. In charge of this elaborate celebration were P. Nadolski, Charles Wolski, Peter Coda, John Ziemski and V. Manak.

St. Adalbert's

By 1912 the members of the congregation felt that there was a real need to erect a school to educate the younger members of the parish. A succession of fundraisers were held to help acquire the $16,000 necessary to pay for a building. Members of the parish were creative. Several bazaars were held at the East End Music Hall and Euclid (Almo) Hotel, with everything from a gold watch to an automobile being auctioned to the highest bidder. James Bardon donated two building lots, located in the vicinity of the new St. Joseph's Orphanage. All the funds to build this small school were raised through the hard work of such families as the Codas, Nadolski, Urbaniaks, and Pietrowskis.

In June of 1916 Kenneth Crumpton was chosen as the architect for the new school. The building, to be constructed by the firm of Sherrick and Johnson, was 70 feet by 50 feet, contained three classrooms, a basement auditorium/gymnasium and living quarters for the Sisters. The work was under the supervision of several members of the parish including Stanislaus Kosmatka, Joseph Polakowski, Frank Cieslicki, and Theodore Meronek as well as Father Jazdzewski.

Finally, on August 20, 1916, the cornerstone was laid. Five hundred people were present to hear Father Jazdzewski, Father F. T. Schulz of Duluth, and Father C.J. Weber, vice chancellor of the Superior diocese, speak about the importance of a Catholic education. The cornerstone, which contained the names of the parishioners, names of the contributors to the building fund, and the clergymen present, was put in

Superior Catholics

place and work proceeded on the structure.

Fundraising continued after the laying of the cornerstone in order to raise the final few dollars necessary to finish the school. At last, on September 4, 1917, the building was completed and Bishop J.M. Koudelka was present to take part in its dedication. Following a mass and a dinner served by the women of the church, a picnic was held by the congregation on the banks of the Nemadji River. That fall St. Adalbert's School opened its doors to 100 pupils and began the task of educating the children of Superior's Polish immigrants. Through the years such memorable people as Father Francis Nowak, Sister Mary Digna, Sister Maurice, and Father Oswald Gasper would touch the lives of the students of St. A's. Under the watchful eyes of the Sisters of St. Francis of the Congregation of Our Lady of Lourdes and the Sisters of St. Joseph, this small Polish school continued its task of educating the children of East End and Allouez until it closed forever in 1965.

St. Adalbert's

Tribute to Father Nowak

In 1919 a newly ordained priest named Father Francis Nowak came to be the priest at St. Adalbert's parish. Father Francis Nowak was born in 1892, making him 27 years old when he became a priest at St. Adalbert's.

Father Nowak was a gifted athlete in the Toledo, Ohio area where he came from, and they say that he was such a good baseball player that he had a chance to play professional baseball, but he sacrificed it for the priesthood.

I went to St. Adalbert's from kindergarten to 8th grade, graduating in 1952. In those nine years, I looked at many softballs pitched by Father Nowak who played pitcher for both teams. At noon hour he would pick out the sides and make up two teams and he would pitch and be the umpire and make all the decisions. At noon hour in the winter he'd come down to the gym and he was the referee. For football in the fall at noon hour, he would make up two teams and he was the quarterback. I caught quite a few passes thrown by Father.

We had this huge tree alongside the road in left field. When we played baseball, if the right-handed batters could get hold of a fly ball and hit it up into that tree, they had a pretty good chance of getting on base because the ball would come down on the branches like a pinball machine and it was tough for the fielders to catch it. It was tough for the left-handed batters, which I was one, to ever hit it into the tree.

Superior Catholics

There was a little gully with a lot of deep bushes just beyond the Carter house in right field and if you could reach that, the ball would usually get lost in the deep brush and it was a home run.

Father used to bowl in town evenings and from what I hear he was really a gifted bowler. He was a very talented golfer. I guess just about anything that had to do with sports, Father was right up there.

I remember this baseball that I saw a couple of times sitting on a piano in the front room of Father's house given to him and autographed by the Commissioner of Baseball.

It's been said that he was so well known around the Cleveland area that when the Indians got in the World Series, they sent Father tickets. I know he didn't go. He gave them away to somebody else. He was well thought of and remembered everywhere.

Anybody that ever knew Father knew that he had a great heart for being kind to people. I remember when we'd be playing softball at noon in the street with Father. Many times somebody would come by that was down on their luck, some old timer. Father would stop the game and go over and talk to the fella and dig into his pocket and he'd give him some money so he would have something to eat with. He'd tell one of us to get his housekeeper, Lou, who was also his cousin, and ask her to get a few packs of cigarettes and give them to the guy. The same thing would happen to little kids. He'd stop the game and tell someone to go get Lou and give them some candy bars.

I use to serve Mass for Father Nowak and I had a

St. Adalbert's

partner named Johnny Ruks. In the summer after a full week of serving, Father would say after Mass, "Boys, I'm going downtown today. Go on out there and check the tires on the car." So we'd have to go out there and walk around the car and check the tires and come back and tell Father it was okay. Father said he would like some company. I'll tell you to walk down Tower Avenue was really something. To walk two blocks took twenty to twenty-five minutes because everybody was stopping him. If the guy ever ran for public office God help the guy who ran against him. They wouldn't have had a chance!

I remember one Christmas I was chosen to serve midnight Mass with Father Nowak and it was really an experience. They had extra chairs in the aisles all the way from the front to the back of the church and they had chairs until we ran out of chairs up on the altar and there were people standing by the altar. When we served there was a lot of pressure because there were just little paths around the altar to do what you were supposed to do. It was really warm —so many bodies in that church. The place was probably filled to double capacity. Nowadays I don't think the fire codes would ever stand for it. It was just amazing how many people turned out for Father Nowak's midnight Mass.

Father Nowak passed away in 1964 and is buried in the priest's circle at Calvery Cemetery just off Highway 105 on the outskirts of Superior.

— **Mike Stranko**

Superior Catholics

MEMORIES OF ST. ADALBERT'S

Shame and a big stick - those were the primary tools of discipline of the nuns who taught me. One nun in particular, Sister B., aka "Benji", was the worst in my experience. She used a rope as a whip, a large stick, and her own hands which were as big as hams. In the seventh or eighth grade a few of us decided to organize against her and hid her stick until the day of the PTA meeting. We went as a small group and presented it to some of the women of the PTA. The end. Nothing more was heard about it, nothing was done. Benji just got another stick.

In the 7th grade I had my worst experience. Religion was taught as the first class of the day, right after mass. Benji said, "Take out your missals." I rolled my eyes and opened my desk to get my missal. The next thing I remember is standing in the hall with Benji yelling and sputtering and calling me audacious! I didn't know what it meant but looked it up later. Then came that ham size hand sharply against my cheek. I knew my head spun and I probably cried. When we went outside for recess, I went home and told my mom what had happened and that I was "not going back to that school." Of course, I returned to school at lunch time. Nothing more was ever said. I don't remember what my mother said. There was always that sense that somehow what the nuns did was okay because our parents never did anything about it.

— Toni Cummings Gotelaere

St. Adalbert's

I revered the Sisters of St. Joseph of the Third Order of St. Francis, who, from 1951-1959, guided me at St. Adalbert's. Sister Benitia influenced me in the later grades —so much so, in fact, that I have gone more than once to the convent in Stevens Point to visit her grave. On my first visit, when I asked the convent archivist where Sister Benitia's grave might be found in the small cemetery on the grounds, she said, "Oh, Benitia is very near to St. Joseph." And that is where I found Sister Benitia that beautiful June afternoon —beneath the statue of St. Joseph, whose outspread arms will shade and protect her always. Sister Benitia, the former Gisella Kerkes, was born January 6, 1898 and died September 4, 1984. "Go with God."

In the 1950s when I was a child, Father Francis Nowak, our beloved parish priest, came to houses near the Feast of the Epiphany to write "K.M.B." in chalk over the door. The initials were the Three Wise Men's —Kasmir, Melchior, and Balthasar. Having forgotten the lovely custom when Father Nowak died in 1963 —when my travels took me away from home for many years— I warmly and vividly recalled it one afternoon when I saw, written in chalk above the door of a German restaurant in Denver, Colorado, "K.M.B." Thirty years had passed since I, a boy, saw the letters Father Nowak had written above the door of my parents' home.

— **Anthony Bukoski**

Superior Catholics

I remember the little old Polish lady that used to clean at St. Adalbert's. She lived on 27th and 5th Street. She was the sweetest person.

I had an aunt that was a nun and her friend was teaching first, second and third grade at St. Adalbert's. There was no kindergarten and the nun told my mother, "Just send Joyce. She can come to school." There were three big statues in the corner of the lower grades room and I went to school and played behind those statues all day.

— Joyce Lier

They used to have a tennis court in back of St. Adalbert's and we played at recess and after school. I went to St. Francis in first and second grade. I couldn't speak English and Laura McMann sat next to me. She was very nice and helped me learn English. I don't know what I would have done without her.

We had a program at St. Adalbert's once. I played the piano with my sister Pauline and my brother Anthony played the violin and we were all playing a different tune. Our mother was in the audience and she was very embarrassed.

— Angeline Bronson

Being an altar boy at St. Adalbert's was quite a challenge. If you were a boy, you were expected to at least try out when you reached the 4th grade.

St. Adalbert's

Training was pretty tough for a 9 or 10-year-old kid. Not only did you have to learn all of the routines, you had to memorize all of the responses. And in 1959 that meant doing it in Latin.

As I recall, there were only three guys in my 4th grade class that took up the challenge to be an altar boy. There was Pat Rookey, Dennis Jaros and myself.

After a few months of rather intense training in the classroom, we were ready for our first Mass. If you are shy, don't become an altar boy. Being up front during a Mass is one of the scariest things I've ever had to do—just knowing that there are some one hundred plus people behind you, watching your every move. Especially knowing that God is watching and worse, the nuns are watching every move you make.

Fortunately, your rookie year you only have to serve at High Mass. At a High Mass, there were usually four altar boys. Two old pros (usually the 7th and 8th graders) and two trainees. The older kids do all the work and the two younger ones just spend the whole time either kneeling or sitting. After a few masses were under your belt (or cassocks), you could relax enough to actually mutter some of the words that the two older kids are rattling off at about a hundred miles an hour.

Then, after spending about six months getting all this Latin down, the Pope decides it's time to let everyone say the Mass in "vernacular". Now this is a big word for a kid in the 4th grade.

As time went by, we all learned the Mass responses

Superior Catholics

in English. And, I became an "old pro". Then summer came. Of course, there were still daily Masses and someone had to get up and be there. Usually there were two of us there to handle this. Summertime was just a time to practice and perfect your skills and become the perfect altar boy. Fortunately, there was a schedule so you wouldn't have to do it everyday.

I remember the first time I had to solo. I was in 5th grade and it was a Saturday in late summer. I was fairly calm about it at first. It only took me three tries to get all twenty buttons on my cassock to line up right. Then, of course, I couldn't find any matches to light the altar candles and I lit my wick from one of the votive candles to accomplish this. Finally it was time to go out into the sacristy. There were only a dozen or so people in the church, but it may as well have been a hundred. My nervousness was quite apparent to Father Nowak. He just told me to relax and he would help me over the rough spots. I just knew if I screwed up I was going to have a spot reserved for me in Hell (or at least in the very bottom of Purgatory). Well, I survived that day relatively error-free and many more such days over the next few years.

After that day, every challenge in life was a piece of cake. Because, when you screw up in life, nobody cares. When you screw up as an altar boy, you know that God and all the Saints are watching. And, I think sometimes they're there helping you through it as well.

— **Larry Lier**

St. Adalbert's

It was a very cold day. Mass had started. A dog wandered into the church. Some men tried to grab the dog and take it out. Father Nowak turned around and said, "Let the dog stay. He's cold too."

— Rose Corcoran Bogan

The nuns did many tasks besides teaching. They instructed and trained us to work diligently at home and school. They took care of Father's vestments, led the choir and trained the altar boys for serving at Mass every day of the week."Bez pracy nie ma Kotaczy." Without work there is no bread.

— Annie Snyder

I graduated from St. Adalbert's in 1946. During the last few years while attending this school I was a member of Father Nowak's grade school basketball team. Father Nowak had brought in Stanley (Moose) Davidowski, a man from the East End area, to assist him in coaching the basketball team. Moose taught us quite a few things about ball handling and shooting. At that time Superior East High School had the 7th and 8th grades attending that school, and they had a basketball team made up from these two grades, and the team was known as the "future first 5" of East High School. It was arranged for us to scrimmage this highly rated 7th and 8th grade team in a regular type game at East High School gymnasium which was like a field-house to us. We went up there and beat them.

Superior Catholics

Julius Juel, who was their coach at the time, was very upset getting beat by this little Catholic grade school, know as "Potato College", from East End. But that's the way it was with Father Nowak's basketball teams. He turned out some good ones.

— **Jim Stranko**

I remember when I was attending St. Adalbert's grade school in the mid 1940's an occasional snowstorm would hit the area. In those days there was no such thing as school buses, especially in the Catholic grade school system. When the storm was just starting Father Nowak would show up at school because he was worried about the little kids getting home. So before the storm got too bad, Father would put as many lower grade kids in the car that he could fit and run them home. Sometimes he would have to make 3 or 4 trips before all the necessary little kids were taken care of. The only older ones who got to go were those that lived in the country. The rest of us 6th, 7th and 8th graders were old enough to fend for ourselves. Sometimes if the storm didn't get too bad, the older kids might stay in school all day.

— **Jim Stranko**

This is a story about how our short-cut to St. Adalbert's School came to an end. This took place in the early 1920's when I was about 11 years old. A good number of us kids used to live on the

St. Adalbert's

other side of the 25th Avenue East tracks from St. Adalbert's School. We lived in the East 3rd Street area and, of course, would take the shortest path we could to school, which was across the park and over a little 2 foot wide concrete bridge over Newton Creek in the 3rd Street area. One day this lady who lived on the hill in the area where we crossed said she didn't want us using that trail anymore. It wasn't her land-it probably belonged to the city but it was the way she was. Being kids we just kept on going that shortcut. Then one day she bought a cow and put it on the hillside. One day when we were taking our usual shortcut to school the cow started running at us like it was chasing us and we all took off liked scared rabbits across the creek. But being scared little kids we never went that way again for fear of the cow - and we always took the long way around. End of shortcut and end of story.

— **Mary Zawin Stranko**

We were serving Mass back when we had devotion on Sunday afternoon. Father said, "I'm going to take you boys swimming after devotions." We got in his car and he took us out to Eau Claire Lakes. As soon as we got out of town Father took his hat off and his coat off and took out a big cigar. We had never seen Father without a collar and with a big stogie in his mouth. When we got to Eau Claire Lakes we put on our suits and everything and Father put oil all over his body and it kept him kinda warm so he

Superior Catholics

didn't feel the cold water. The water was like ice. He went in and he kept saying, "Come on boys, the water is so nice." We never got passed our ankles because our feet felt like they stiffened up in the water. We never did go in. Before we got back, he put his collar back on, put his hat on, and that's the end of the story.

— **Frank Zawin**

At noon Father Nowak would come down to the gym for an hour/hour and a half. Father would play basketball with us. He really ran up us and down the floor. We all wore long underwear. We really got hot and sweaty. The bell rang, and we went up in the room, and the nun was really angry. It was the middle of winter, and it was cold, and she went around and opened all the windows and we were freezing, but that was life with Father Nowak. He loved sports and the nuns could not say anything about it.

Everyone in Superior loved Father. No matter what religion they belonged to. When we used to serve devotions on Sunday afternoons, he always took us servers in his car and he drove uptown to Guenard's, and he always treated us with a bag of popcorn. But what got to me was we would walk down Tower Avenue with Father and his politeness. He would be waving. If it was a woman, he'd tip his hat to her. He waved at every car.

— **Frank Zawin**

St. Adalbert's

This story is about a tattletale. We had one nun who started with us in the third grade. That was the last grade in that room with only three rooms in the school and how happy we were that we were going onto a new room and a new nun. Lo and behold we got into the fourth grade and there she was.

We had these little girls who were trying to make points with the nuns. We were just innocent school kids that would get together on weekends and we'd be playing around. The girls gave the nuns the names of all of us and said they were playing love and marriage and when we got to school the next day believe me she gave a talk and went on and on. After that she wouldn't talk to us. She wouldn't correct our papers. So we had to go and talk to her and apologize for something we didn't do.

At the end of the 6th grade, we were so happy that we didn't have to put up with her and we go to the third room that is the seventh grade and lo and behold there she was and she stayed with us all the way through the eighth grade and we were a very unhappy bunch and some of us were apologizing continually to her, but we all came out of it and I hope she's okay.

— **Frank Zawin**

All the boys played basketball at lunch. The gym was hot and a friend of mine used to sweat a lot. When we got back to the room Sister used to tell him to stop sweating. Of course he couldn't, so she hit him. This went on all during basketball season.

— **Tom Meronek**

Superior Catholics

I remember being on the playground on a very cold day. Father was out there, too. He was wearing a long, black wool coat. An old man came by. He was not wearing a coat. The man stopped to talk to Father. Father removed his coat and put it on the old man.

— **Georgeann Cheney**

I spent seven years at St. St. Adalbert's. I remember three grades in each classroom—desks nailed to the floor—nuns living in an apartment right in the school—the beautiful statues in church. We had a statue of the Virgin Mary that had a wreath of white lights around her head in a halo. It was my favorite.

I spent many years at St. Adalbert's diagramming sentences.

No one has ever asked me to do this in real life, but if they do, I'm ready.

I left Catholic school in eighth grade and went to East High School. The first day of class my math teacher, Mr. Roesch, asked me a question and I stood up immediately and answered, "Yes, Sister." Everyone laughed. I had been trained to always stand when spoken to by a teacher. I never did it again. Embarrassment can be a very good teacher, too.

— **Georgeann Cheney**

I remember being a teacher's pet along with Mary Ann Lambert. We used to run errands a lot for the nuns. Mary Ann and I spent a great deal of time in

St. Adalbert's

the basement of the school bundling newspapers for paper drives. It was great fun!

— **Carol Smith**

I remember the nun we had in 7th grade would always say, "Boys are psst" and she would spit! It's a wonder any of us ever went out on dates.

I also remember I stopped throwing up in the morning when I left Catholic school and went on to a public high school.

— **C. H.**

Father Nowak used to come in and give us word games. The prizes were very nice. He used to buy rings for the girls. He would put the first letter of a word or words up on the board and draw dashes for the rest of the letters. Then he would give clues and everyday he would give another clue until someone guessed the word or words. I won this ring for AURORA BOREALIS. I think my dad helped me.

— **Toni Cummings Gotelaere**

My Dad, Frank Cieslicki, took care of the furnace in the school. He would get up at four in the morning before he went to work and stoke the fire. He also made the form for the Sacred Heart statue and put it up on the church lawn.

— **Helen Cummings**

Superior Catholics

My first memory of St. Adalbert's School is of Sister Frumentia, who would be my first, second, and third grade teacher. How do I describe Sister Frumentia? Well, you could say she was fleet of foot and fast of hand. She wielded a mean ruler and wasn't afraid to use it on anyone. She was also quite a storyteller. She scared the heck out of me with her stories of snakes in beds, people being buried alive and what happens to children who don't go to Sunday Mass. I remember her as being quite old, but maybe she just seemed that way to a first grader. She used to fall asleep during reading class, and this proved to be quite a dilemma for her students. You would have to read out loud until Sister told you to stop and if she was asleep you could end up reading a whole book!

I remember her classroom as being warm, with red geraniums in green pots on the windowsill, and the cupboard where she kept all her supplies. Those supplies consisted mostly of score sheets from Waletzko's Bowling Alley. They made great drawing paper! I also remember her keeping a bucket in the cupboard. I think it was a scrub pail, but at the end of the school year she would use it for Kool-Aid. Our treat, just before school ended for the year, was to drink Kool-Aid and play bingo for prizes such as holy cards and statues. Gambling, but with a religious twist.

I remember Sister Tarcilia coming to the 4th and 5th grade room to tell us that President Kennedy had died. The news was shocking, but my most vivid memory is remembering Sister standing against the

St. Adalbert's

door with tears rolling down her cheeks. I had never seen a nun cry!

I remember the merry-go-round that Father Oswald put up for us. It was our one piece of playground equipment. That first afternoon, after it was in place, kids were dropping like flies. Everyone learned a lesson that day - you can only go around in a circle for so long before your lunch comes back up.

I remember that we always had elaborate Christmas programs. One year Sister Frumentia made us costumes out of crepe paper and we all had to dance the polka! How appropriate for a Polish school. I remember other years when we put on plays or sang carols. Does anyone have photos from those times? I would love to see them.

I remember my two favorite teachers, Sister Vincent and Sister Therese. They were both young and had new ideas about teaching. Sister Vincent had us listen to the radio to learn geography. I still remember the song about longitude and latitude. Sister Therese always had us doing special projects that were so different from anything else I had ever done in Catholic school. After all these years I still think of her as one of my best teachers.

I remember staying after school to clean blackboards and then going out behind the building to clean the erasers.

I remember hot lunch. What a treat! The smells coming from the kitchen would almost drive you crazy. How did any of us manage to wait until lunchtime? We always had the same menu - sloppy joes,

Superior Catholics

hot dogs, potato chips, cake or jello with little dabs of whipping cream on top and chocolate milk. Has anything since then ever tasted so good?

I remember singing in the choir and waiting for someone to get in trouble for spitting over the choir loft. I always thought the best time to be a part of the choir was on Holy Saturday. Coming into church, the statues would be covered with cloths and everything would be so somber. About halfway through the service, the lights in the church would be turned off and everyone in the congregation would be holding a lit candle. What a view from the choir! And then, when the lights were turned back on, the statues would be uncovered, there would be flowers and candles everywhere and everything would be so bright and joyful. Wasn't St. Adalbert's a beautiful church?

I remember being a crossing guard and wearing a yellow raincoat when it rained.

I remember always having to wear a hat or scarf to church.

I remember having to to sit with our hands behind our backs in Sister Frumentia's class.

I remember Sister Therese playing baseball with us. I can still she her black veil flowing behind her as she ran from base to base.

I remember when the air raid siren would go off and we would have to crouch under our desks and pray it was just a warning and that the Russians really weren't coming after us this time. I still panic when I hear that siren.

I remember eating breakfast in the classroom af-

St. Adalbert's

ter going to Communion at daily Mass. It usually consisted of a cold peanut butter on toast sandwich, fruit cocktail and warm milk.

I remember all the kids from St. Joseph's.

I remember spending a lot of time in church.

I remember Father Nowak always out walking with Lou when we had recess. He always had candy.

I remember the nice cook who gave us cookies.

But most of all I remember my friends - Mary Ann, Liz, Carolyn, Kathy and Katie. Still friends today and the best part of going to Catholic school.

— Teddie Meronek

For some strange reason, I remember only a few school related things.

Diagramming sentences!!! For four years it seemed that it was the only thing that we did. When I got to high school, my freshman year was spent doing the same thing, except that then it was new to the rest of the students. I think that that had a bad influence on the rest of my education. I was bored.

I also remember having to get up in front of the class and having to read poetry and God forbid if you didn't slur at a comma and punctuate a period. You'd have to do it over and over again until it was correct.

I remember standing in the corner of the room for hours, pulling out the encyclopedias to the edge of the shelf and then pushing them back in. I don't ever remember why I was sent to the corner.

I remember singing a song in front of the school at

Superior Catholics

the end of the year graduation when I was in second grade. It was called "I'm Just an Old Man (They Call Me Grandpa)". University students came to school to do my makeup which consisted of powder in my hair to make it gray.

I also remember that there was a tonette band. Twenty kids playing the same thing on their black tonettes. The nuns made blue hats and capes out of crepe paper. They had gold round seals on the hats. The funny thing was that there was a very long music stand that went across the length of the stage. It was made by Leo Meronek.

I remember Sister Maurice playing the organ, badly, and singing even worse.

I remember serving Mass daily even during the summer, except during the summer when I visited my grandmother. I'm sure that I saw more funerals than any ten-year-old alive. I also remember going to what we called the "Crazy House" out in the county to serve Mass for Father Nowak. I think it was a home for people with mental problems. It was in a sort of strange room in which a temporary altar was set up and the people were constantly walking around. It was really scary. I think we went there once a month.

Most of all I remember shoveling the walks and mowing the lawn. I couldn't have been more than 11 and I remember mowing the lawn weekly in the summer with a push mower.

I remember scrubbing the classroom floors with lye so they would be white before they were waxed.

I remember polishing the candlesticks, especially

St. Adalbert's

before a big occasion. I remember the nuns heating the votive lamps with the flame of a candle and then wiping them out with tissue paper.

I remember how terrifying it was to light the very tall candles on the altar. It wasn't until I was an adult that I realized that I had no depth perception and in order to light the candles I had to touch them on the sides and work my way up to the top.

My most vivid memory is being 10 or 11 and having to wash the windows at the parsonage. There I was standing on the top of a very large stepladder trying to clean the bay window using glass wax and a newspaper. You put the glass wax on liquid and it dried to a white haze and then you had to wipe it off with newspaper because it made the glass shine. And there stood the priest's housekeeper, Lou, screaming that I wasn't getting the corners of the windows clean enough.

Curiously, I remember some of the art projects that we did. I think Sister Maurice was really a very good artist. She always had great paintings on the cloakroom doors. And it amazed me when she painted the statues. Anyway, she had interesting projects for her classes to do. Once we made waste baskets out of cardboard and Christmas wrapping paper. Once we made these strange flowers that I'd never seen. They were hyacinths and we made them out of crepe paper. I remember coloring pictures of birds that were copied with purple lines on a hectograph or something like that. It now seems peculiar that I don't ever remember seeing some of those birds we had to read

Superior Catholics

a description on how to color them. During the Christmas season I still remember coloring the pictures of Baby Jesus and trying to get the colors soft and smooth and Janice Coda always did it better. She would use a tissue to smooth out the colors and Sister Maurice always made it a point to point it out to the rest of the class.

— Ed Lambert

Every Saturday my dad would bring coal to Father Nowak. My dad was superintendant of the coal dock in Allouez. We would drag gunnysacks of coal to his house. He would give me tons of Milky Way candy bars that probably cost more than the coal.

— George Sheridan

I started St. Adalbert's School in the first grade in 1948 and graduated from the eighth grade in 1956. I lived a half block away on 23rd Avenue East and many of my neighborhood friends also went there. My first memory was of the teeter-totter. I got on one end and my good friend Bob McNaughton got on the other. I went up so fast my end hit someone and they got hurt but I can't remember who. First, second, and third grades were in the same room - 101 - and our teacher was Sister Rose Mary. All of our little desks were fastened to wood strips on the floor. First graders sat by the window on 23rd Avenue and I liked to watch the tracked sidewalk plows, flag, traffic, and the old brown building across the street. My favorite

St. Adalbert's

time was recess when we had snacks and milk from those little glass bottles. Sister was very strict and you were in big trouble for not doing your work. We learned how to line up and march to church, into school, or anywhere else we went as a group. We went to Mass every morning before school - grades 1-3 sat in front on the right. The upper grades sat on the left. We were studying for Holy Communion after which the boys would serve mass and the girls would sing in the choir. Sister Maurice would play the organ and lead the choir. The boys would memorize all of the prayers in Latin. It would be years before I actually understood them. The fourth and fifth grades in my class were with Sister Thaddeus in room 102. Things were really tough there. I still can't diagram sentences very well, but I haven't practiced for quite a while. I think most of us were heavy into playing marbles behind the school during recess. The double features at the East End Show House were super. In the sixth grade we moved to room 103 and Sister Maurice. We regarded her as the ultimate authoritarian. She quickly verified this when I got caught drawing a dogfight between F 86 saber jets and Mig 15's over Korea. My dreams of being a pilot or artist were quickly over as I had to spend the rest of the year writing penalties hundred of times and reducing fractions. We also had lots of charts on the wall with stars, but I can't remember if it was for good or bad work. For the seventh and eighth grades we had a new teacher in the school - Sister Angela. We were the upper classmen and finally it was our turn to rule the

Superior Catholics

school. Sister Angela had a different idea, so we let her think that she was running things. My mother got a job as custodian at the school, so she was able to keep pretty close tabs on what I was doing. Sister would always tell her how wonderful I was. Everyone now had TV sets and we all went "television crazy." I can't remember how many years we will have to spend in Purgatory for watching all that TV. I just hope we all make it there. Father Nowak was a real life saint. He called all of us his boys and girls. Adults were all "my friend." He always had a wave, smile, candy, money or cigar for everyone. He and his old Ford were the school bus for the lucky kids who lived in Allouez. At noon there was always a softball or basketball game for the upper grades. Everyone played or watched. Everyone knew everyone else in the school. Father was the pitcher, umpire, or referee and he always kept everything even. We played softball on 3rd Street. The big willow tree was on the edge of left field and you were out if you hit the house in right field. Basketball was in our little gym. Everyone wore socks. There wasn't enough room to dribble, and whenever everyone, trying to get at the person with the ball, caused the herd to stop, Father called a jump ball. We played in the Catholic School League and in spite of being the smallest school, we always did quite well. I still remember the blue jackets with the white bars and our name and school that Father bought us for a good season. I served Mass often during the summer because I lived so close to church. Father would always take

St. Adalbert's

us to the Arrow Cafe or give us money for treats. Father's housekeeper, Lou, would keep us on task. During the eighth grade the nuns convinced my mom that I should go to Cathedral High School. All of my buddies were going to East. My Uncle Art made up my mind when he promised to buy me a new 22 if I would go to Cathedral. I did well at Cathedral, but after my uncle passed away, I joined my friends at East for my last three years. I look back on my years at St. Adalbert's and think it was the best option for me. I am a teacher and have been in school for fifty years and I think I needed the discipline and rigor from the nuns and the small, close knit community of our tiny school. I think I learned a great deal from listening and watching the higher classes in each room. I can still recall names and experiences with nearly everyone at the school. These are all good memories. I'm sure time has a lot to do with that, but not as much as Father Nowak. We were blessed.

— **Tom Vengrin**

I was in first grade. We had to count to ten in Polish. I would count and get to three and the nun would hit me. She did this several times. I went home and told my mother. Mother told me to count. I was saying, "One-two-PEE." Pee and three sound alike in Polish.

— **Anonymous**

Superior Catholics

Remember Hot Lunch?

Sloppy Joe recipe from St. Adalbert's *hot lunch!* Make up a batch—get some chips, green Jello and chocolate milk. Take a culinary journey back in time! And don't forget the Sno Balls for desert!

   3 lbs. ground beef 1 - 28 oz. bottle ketchup 1 bunch celery 2 large onions 1/2 tsp. dry mustard 1 tbl. sugar 1/2 tsp. chili powder (optional) Salt & pepper

   Fry ground beef until browned. Fry celery and onion in another pan. Add dry mustard, sugar, ketchup to the above. Simmer 3 hours, or until done.

— Recipe courtesy of Olga LaBoy

Here is a photo of Father Francis Nowak's 25th anniversary Jubilee. It took place on May 1, 1944.

St. Adalbert's

NOTICE.

Every pupil should be on the school premises fifteen minutes before the commencement of school exercises and NOT earlier.

Parents should send **WRITTEN EXCUSES,** when the pupils have been absent or tardy.

Preparation of the next days lessons should follow supper before fatigue comes.   Parents may help by hearing their children recite but should give no special lessons, as the children have enough to do in meeting the requirements of their regular teacher.

Send the children to school every day. Truant playing always begins with parents keeping them at home for some slight cause. See that they are on time, for it is but a step from the tardy scholar to the truant.

Be sure that the children attend their religious duties on Sunday, and that they nave a prayer book or beads. On Confession Day see that they go at the time appointed for them, and not at night when they are in the way of adults, besides contracting the habit of being out of doors after dark.

The Catholic School, for which Priests, Religious teachers and people are sacrificing so much, can effect the good intended only with the co-operation of parents.

Note to parents printed on the back of Georgeann's 3rd grade report card. "...it is but a step from the tardy scholar to the truant."

Sts. Anthony & Margaret

Et cum spiritu tu

This is Rosemarie Ruthgeerts-Birch's First Communion group. The altar in the background was in the Sts. Anthony & Margaret Church.

Superior Catholics

Talk of a school for the children of the Belgian settlers of Allouez began in 1914. That was the year that Father Randolph Hanssens began pursuing his dream of a complete Belgian settlement with the church, school and convent surrounded by the homes of the parish families.

Father Rudolph had very definite ideas about educating boys and girls. He wanted to give his young charges the equivalent of a public school education with the addition of industrial training. He didn't believe in co-education and hoped to eventually raise enough money for separate classrooms and playgrounds for each of the sexes.

So, in July of 1914, Rene Lagae, Allouez builder, began work on a church that would be named for Saints Anthony and Margaret. Father Rudolph had chosen these names because St. Margaret was a favorite Belgian saint and St. Anthony because he was special to the Franciscan order of priests who served the parish. The church was built on property donated by James and Emma Bardon with five additional lots donated by Emma A. Corrigan. When completed, the church cost $4,200.

Father Rudolph left the small Allouez parish in 1917 before his dream of a school was realized. In 1918, Father William J. Kubelbeck picked up where Father Rudolph had left off and immediately began raising money for a rectory and school. Within one year an $8,000 rectory was built and furnished, and the first school fund raising campaign was a success with over $6,000 collected. Within four years the building fund had increased to $12,000 and the dream of a school

Sts. Anthony & Margaret

was moving closer to reality.

In the spring of 1925, the congregation voted unanimously to give their consent to spend $42,000 to build a school. The building, consisting of six classrooms, a gymnasium and auditorium, was designed by John O. Bach and built by contractors Jenson and Campbell.

The school was opened on September 14, 1925 with an enrollment of 98 students. Four grades were taught by the Franciscan Sisters of Perpetual Adoration with four more grades added in 1926. Saints Anthony & Margaret School was formally dedicated and blessed by Bishop Joseph Pinten on October 25, 1925 with the members of the parish holding a celebratory dinner beforehand. Then, it was onto the business of educating the youngsters of Allouez which would continue in this small school until 1969.

Rosemarie Ruthgeert-Birch's First Communion. Is she precious or what?

Superior Catholics

MEMORIES OF STS. ANTHONY & MARGARET

The nuns locked us in after school for something we did. Two of the guys jumped out the window from the second story. I didn't. I may be foolish, but I'm not crazy.

— Hut-a-Butt Gotelaere

How I Remember Joe: I'll never forget his respect for the church. I was always told to tip your hat when passing the church. I always remember Joe Laverdiere whenever he walked by the front sidewalk of the church, he'd lift his hat with one hand and rub the other hand through his hair. It wasn't a "tip" - but I always got "THE MESSAGE".

— Nick Gotelaere

In the second grade at St Anthony's we had to line up for lunch to walk out orderly. The girl in front of me sat behind me—so when we lined up—there she was—lined up right there and I leaned forward and kissed her on the back of her neck.
 I can't remember the rest of the story.

— Nick Gotelaere

I ran home at recess for something I forgot and grabbed a pickle to eat. Back at school it was church

Sts. Anthony & Margaret

day and wondering - do I go to communion or not? If I do I die - I'll go to hell. If I don't the nuns will really make me sorry. I was so scared. I went to communion. I never could confess this to anyone. I was in high school before I realized it was OK that I did this. I was in third or fourth grade.

— Becky Gotelaere Jones

I followed Sister Amanda around. I was her pet. One day I was in the choir loft listening to her and I was late for class. The nun in the classroom said, "Where were you?" I said I was in church with the pricipal. She didn't do anything to me. It's not what you know, it's *who* you know.

— Don Gotelaere

When I was five I got to go to St. Anthony's for a day (or half a day) to visit because I would be in first grade the following year. My brother Bob took me. He was in eighth grade. I was so proud and excited. I remember the room, the desk, Bob sitting behind me and I felt protected and very special. Bob leaned over, gave me a stick of gum and said, "Here, chew this, the nuns love it when you chew gum." I got caught and was yelled at. This wonderful day turned into a frightening experience. Thanks Bob!

— Becky Gotelaere Jones

Superior Catholics

Joe Laverdiere was St. Anthony's. He cared about all the kids - but more than just caring - he let the kids know. He talked to us, he listened to us, he would help us. For four years I helped Joe clean the school after school closing each day. During summer and weekends I mowed lawns, painted classrooms, shoveled snow, filled the coal grawler and whatever. As my sister Becky said, "Joe made up for all the nuns." Nick recalls that he would always remember when Joe walked by the church he would always tip his hat and brush his hair back.

— Steve Gotelaere

My Memories of St. Anthony's

Separate areas for outside recess time. Girls out front in field or cinder covered street. Boys out back in baseball field. Teeter-totters for small ones. Restroom "lavatory" monitors. Students lined up on stairway - single file - no talking.

First Fridays gathering in downstairs hall area. Candy sale each fall. My favorite was hard anise candies.

Christian Conduct

Brown paper covers on school books. End of year we cleaned books with erasers and bleach on Q-Tips. Father Kubelbeck came to each room to distribute report cards.

Father Tracy appeared on the playground with khaki pants and white shirt. Quite untraditional for the 50's.

Sts. Anthony & Margaret

khaki pants and white shirt. Quite untraditional for the 50's.

The nuns lived in the school building. They had the space of what would equal two classrooms. Imagine - five nuns living in such a small area.

The nuns would hang bed sheets outside to dry. The tallest girl in our class was always asked to "help fold" and the dry linen was taken from the clothesline.

Giving and receiving Valentines was a big event. For several years we were encouraged to exchange "holy cards" instead of commercial Valentine cards. I placed my collection in a scrap book. I still have it today.

The grade school choirs sang for funeral masses. We were excused from early morning classes and were well aware of the solemn service in which we participated.

The school building and grounds were always very clean. The janitor's name was Joe Laverdiere. Everyone knew him, liked him, and respected him. We knew of our roles in keeping the school neat and clean. Fire drills were always taken seriously, but there always seemed to be a sense of excitement as we left the building.

I think school pictures were taken every other year. We sat at our desks, arms folded on top of the writing surface. I still have some of the pictures.

The "Crowning of the May Queen" was celebrated in May. Must have been about Mother's Day or First Communion. One of the eighth grade girls was dressed in an old wedding dress, the younger girls marched in

Superior Catholics

procession and threw rose petals. All the "Virgin Mary" hymns were sung.

Lent, Holy Week and the celebration of Easter were a part of school. We had Lenten banks, gave up candy and movies, the statues were covered with purple cloths.

One day (8th grade 1953), a fellow classmate came back from lunch. He was late and all eyes were on him as he entered the room. He proudly announced "Stalin is dead." We had no radios or TV in the school, so international news was not instantly available.

There were two large swinging doors through which you entered St. Anthony's Church proper from the back vestibule. There must have been a two inch clearance between the doors. Anyone arriving late for Mass would peer through the opening, hoping to sneak into church while people were standing, figuring we would not be noticed quite so much.

Classmates that I graduated with from the 8th grade at St. Anthony's School:

        Janice DeSmet
        Kathleen Plachta
        Evonne DeMal
        Joan Soderlund
        Rose Parenteau
        Helen LaVoy
        Jeanne Durst
        Elaine Smith
        Marie Lois Ruthgeerts
        Paul DeCook
        Richard Vergauwen

Sts. Anthony & Margaret

Dexter St. George
Jerry Dhooge
Ed O'Brien
Bill DeBock
Warren Gobin
LeRoy Dumonsau

— Barbara Ruthgeerts Byrne

First Grade

My teacher was Sister M. Carmel, a little tiny woman - an F.S.P.A. - Franciscan Sister of Perpetual Adoration. We learned to read and print. One of the high points of first grade for me was being chosen, along with two of my classmates, Carol Dens and Joan VanOvermeiren, to be the train bearers for the girl from eighth grade who was to crown the Blessed Virgin Mary statue in the crowning done every May. The eighth grade girl was Shirley Miller and she wore the traditional bridal dress and veil, and Joan, Carol and myself were in floor-length formals. Mine was pink, worn previously by my cousin when she was flower girl for my mother's wedding. We practiced alot, walking slowly, pretending to carry the train, and being impressed by the eighth grade girls, members of the court.

Also in first grade I had my first experience in the theater. A production of "Snow White and the Seven Dwarfs" was staged in the St. Anthony gym, along

Superior Catholics

with Cinderella for the seventh and eighth grade girls. I played the part of Dopey (a non-speaking part).

Grade Two

The biggest event in second grade was making our First Communion. We prepared for many weeks, learning prayers, songs, how to process in, keep your hands folded, receive the host on our tongue, swallow it without chewing it first and to present our best selves to Jesus. I can remember Sister Victoria telling us "No matter where it itches, don't scratch". During this preparation time the "public school kids" came to our school and spent two weeks or so with us so they could get in all the practices. This was a very exciting time for all of us. I received my First Communion on May 29, 1949.

I have our class picture.

Grades Three & Four

Sister M. Verena was my teacher both years. I especially remember Valentine Holy Card exchange in those two years. We did not exchange store-bought cards but holy picture cards that the sisters sold for one penny up to five or ten cents each. I think the money went to the missions. We had the usual decorated box in the front of the room and Sister was the person who distributed the cards to each of us as we sat at our desks. My sister Barbara and I placed our cards in scrapbooks to be looked at and enjoyed and of course the favorite ones were put in our daily missals that we carried to Mass every day. I still have my album of holy picture Valentine cards.

Sts. Anthony & Margaret

Grades Five and Six

Sister Coronata was a firm believer in "Silence is golden", diagramming sentences, and learning poetry "by heart". We had special days when Sister read and explained the poem and then assigned us lines to remember. Then we had races to see who could recite fastest. The Village Blacksmith and In Flanders Fields still stick in my mind.

Sixth grade year we all composed questions and answers concerning a wide range of subjects to be submitted to KDAL Radio for a quiz program they had on the air at the time. Myself and another classmate, Ruth Pellitier were chosen as contestants. We were on the program on a Saturday morning and one of the questions that I was asked was one I wrote! I won a quart of ice cream.

Grades Seven and Eight

Sister M. Amanda was the teacher for these grades. Sister loved to sing, play the piano and organ and loved dramatics.

In the eighth grade we had a play in the spring of the year "The Ghost and Mr. Penney".

And in seventh grade it was a musical - but I can't remember the name.

Sister had us plan an unheard of activity - a St. Cecelia Day dance and party. We had music and refreshments, it was in the evening. We all "dressed up".

She also got the Home & School Association to buy a movie projector and she showed us Shirley Temple films. Remember - very few families had TV

Superior Catholics

then so these movies were a real treat.

Sister also loved baseball and during the World Series she brought the school radio, a large wooden box-like affair, and we listened to the games and did "projects" that could be accomplished while listening to the play-by-play.

Sister Amanda also took our class to the Shrine Parade in downtown Superior. It was the State Convention City and a really big parade was planned. We went on the city bus and it was quite an adventure.

Our class had a graduation Mass with a lovely breakfast after the ceremony. Sister was the person who came up with the idea and was able to be there, but could not eat with us. That was prohibited in 1955. Sisters didn't eat with others. I have a photo of our graduation class.

Our school days started with daily Mass. All school children attending, seated according to grades, girls separate from boys. We were expected to keep silent, kneel up straight - no padded kneelers at St. Anthony's - bare boards - and pay attention to the priest. If we whispered to the child next to us, and Sister saw us, we had to do a written punishment - for first graders numbers from 1-100. I did do numbers a few times.

We walked everywhere in single file - girls first, boys last. We kept silence in the hallways and on the stairways and also in the lavatory, where there were monitors, to make sure of our behavior. They monitored our silence and also made sure we turned the soap dispenser handle once and used one towel to dry our hands. No waste was tolerated.

Sts. Anthony & Margaret

The Sisters were strict but also seemed to like us in a reserved way. There were rules, but I believe we learned alot about life in general by observing the rules. Take turns, do not be proud, be kind to each other, don't waste, pray alot.

During Forty Hours Devotion we all took turns during the school day - I think one-half hour - to be in adoration of the Blessed Sacrament which was exposed in church. Many candles and beautiful flowers adorned the altar and a procession usually led by the Bishop happened during that time. All the children who had received First Communion and could still fit into their dresses/suits were part of the procession. The girls carried roses, and we pulled the petals from the roses and scattered them in the aisle in front of the monstrance being carried by the Bishop, or the parish pastor, under a canopy carried by men of the parish. The incense, candle bearers, flower petals, dressed-up children, the singing and organ music still resound in my mind.

My Graduation Class:
- Carol Dens
- Joan VanOvermeiren
- Yvonne Cheselski
- Joyce LaPorte
- Jean Hoffman
- Marjorie Brunette
- Rosemarie Ruthgeerts
- May Kay Fitzgerald
- Rudy LaJoie

Superior Catholics

David Revoy
Paul DeBeir

— Rosemarie Ruthgeerts Birch

Rosemarie's Good Conduct card. Is she precious or what?

A few of us guys got caught goofing around in eighth grade and Sister said we all had to write 500 times that we were sorry about what we did. We went to the drug store and bought some carbon paper and then we all went to Grandma Bridge's house and started writing using the carbon paper. We handed it in to Sister the next day. She said we didn't have to write it over, but we all had to take it home for our parents to sign it. Our parents found out about what we did and about the carbon paper. Score - Sister 1, the guys zero.

— Tom Lozon

Sts. Anthony & Margaret

First Colmmunion procession.

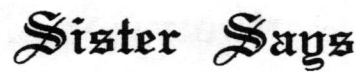

𝕮𝖆𝖙𝖍𝖊𝖉𝖗𝖆𝖑

Deo gratias

Cathedral High School

Superior Catholics

The history of Cathedral School is really the history of two schools - Sacred Heart and St. Joseph's. In 1923 these two parishes merged to become Cathedral of Christ the King and Cathedral School - the only remaining parochial school left in Superior. On October 5, 1890, the school of the Sacred Heart of Jesus, located at 12th Street and John Avenue, was dedicated. The first teachers were the Sisters of St. Joseph from St. Paul, but they were soon replaced by the Franciscan Sister of LaCrosse. The parish continued to grow and by 1908, a new, large brick structure was built at 13th Street and John Avenue. Because the parish church was in such poor repair, services were now conducted on the upper floor of this new building, while the lower floor and all the rooms in the old structure at 12th Street and John Avenue were used for school purposes. St. Joseph's Parish was established in 1896. In the spring of that years, a $10,000 two-story building was constructed at 11th Street and Catlin Avenue. This structure served as both church and school for the German settlers of St. Joseph's. It was later moved to 1418 Baxter Avenue. By 1923 the new Cathedral of Christ the King was completed and these two parishes, St. Joseph's and Sacred Heart, were merged to become one. However, the Cathedral Parish still utilized the school buildings of the two congregations. The first six grades were taught in the building at 12th Street and John Avenue, the seventh and eighth grades at 1418 Baxter Avenue and the high school at 13th Street and John Avenue. By the late 1940's, it was evident that a

Cathedral

new Cathedral School was needed. In 1946, the old St. Joseph's School was razed, and the pupils were moved to the newly completed basement of Cathedral of Christ the King. By August of 1950, ground was broken for the new school and in less than two years, on May 15, 1952, the building was dedicated by Bishop Albert Meyer. The new school was designed by Hansen and Dobberman. When it opened, 500 elementary students were housed on the first two floors and 385 high school student in twelve classrooms on the third floor. The building also included a gymnasium, two locker and shower rooms, a coach's office and storage rooms. The staff consisted of twenty-nine nuns, four priests and coach Steve Bachand. Cathedral continued to offer high school courses until 1969, when it was merged with Superior Senior High and still offers a parochial education to the elementary students of Superior.

Superior Catholics

MEMORIES OF SACRED HEART, ST. JOSEPH'S & CATHEDRAL SCHOOLS

I remember those horrid green, red and brown plaid uniforms we had to wear. The material was so heavy and stiff—I felt like a walking drape. I remember Wednesday mornings. Everyone would whine as we lined up and Sister checked to be sure none of us had gum. Then we would march in silence like miniature soldiers across the street—off to church again. I remember Girl Scout meetings after school. We would laugh, eat treats and make crafts. I laughed so much Mrs. Henning gave me the nickname "Gigglefritz." I ate so many treats I got a bellyache, and I made such a mess making crafts I ended up with glue in my hair. I remember my rebellious tomboy days. I would fight with the boys and tease the girls. A trip to the principal's office cured me fast. I thought I was going to Hell for sure! I remember religion class. One year, during Lent, we colored pictures of the Stations of the Cross. I was so proud of myself when I discovered the color magenta that I made Jesus' clothes magenta in every picture. I remember my bad habit. I would constantly twist and curl my waist-length hair between my fingers. Mrs. Snyder got quite annoyed with me because I was distracted during class. She made me wear metal clips in my hair, sit on my hands and wanted me to put my hair in a ponytail or braid. Mrs. Snyder got more and more frustrated with me, but nothing worked. I remember the year head

Cathedral

lice invaded our school. Everyone had to be checked. We were led one by one down the hall to a tiny room. Two ladies with extra long toothpicks poked and examined our scalps. I started to sweat as I waited for the big announcement. In fifth grade, being told you had head lice was like being diagnosed with a deadly disease. I gasped in horror and then started crying when I found out I had "the bug". I hung my head in shame as I waited for my mom to pick me up. As it turns out, I had such a bad case of head lice that I ended up getting my hair cut really short. I never said anything, but I'm certain Mrs. Snyder is responsible for planting "the bug" in my hair. It was the only thing that cured my bad habit.

— **Anna Larson**

I was in the fifth grade playing in the gym with a friend of mine. He was sort of a troublemaker. He fell and really sliced open his head. I took him back up to the room. He was bleeding a lot. The nun told me to get him out of there. She didn't want that "bad blood" on her floor.

— **Mike Duffy**

Senior year biology class we had to hand in notebooks that were thirty percent of our grade. Sister was asking for our notebooks and the grades we got on them. Mike Duffy said, "I lost it, but I think I got a B-". Sister gave him the B and an A- in the

Superior Catholics

course. She said, "Rick, where's your notebook?" I told her I lost it. She said, "An F for you, sir." Mike was an athlete and Sister loved athletes. I wasn't one and ended up flunking the course. Mike could charm people even then.

— **Rick Hoglund**

As a freshman going out for football at Cathedral there was never quite enough equipment to go around. Of course the seniors and returning lettermen got the "good stuff" and the freshmen got what was left. Sometimes there wasn't anything left so we had to improvise. For example, Jack Milroy didn't get a practice jersey, so he wore his brother's softball jersey over his shoulder pads. His brother worked on the railroad and the railroad had its own league. The jersey said "Clerks" on the front of it. The coaches and upper classmen called him by that name for quite sometime. As for football shoes, some got 'em, but most freshmen didn't. Tom Bronson was lucky, he got two shoes, both to the same foot and he wore them anyway. He kept running to the left. Dick DeMars wore combat boots and I wore tennis shoes. We had no freshman team, no j.v. team, most of us never got into a game. We never missed practice, got pounded by the varsity in scrimmages, and loved every minute of it. The coaches were Bill Meyers, Steve Bachand, and for the first couple of weeks Len Horyza before he went back to college or the Marine Corps.

— **Dan (Sam) Conway**

Cathedral

In the fall of 1958, I was a sophomore at Cathedral High. One afternoon during lunch period, a fellow classmate offered me a pinch of Copenhagen. I had never experienced the taste of chewing tobacco before. Immediately after placing the tobacco in the back corner of my mouth, the bell rang indicating the lunch period had ended. I went into my first class for the afternoon with saliva continuing to build up in my oral cavity. It would happen that I was the first student to be called on by Sister Alcoa regarding the day's assignment. Unable to answer her question with a mouthful of saliva and tobacco I rushed to the nearest window and opened it to expel the contents in my mouth. The dark matter that I expelled splattered all over the window. This caused quite a disturbance in the classroom. The good Sister became so infuriated, she grabbed me by the ear and personally escorted me down to the principal's office. Needless to say, I have not tried chewing tobacco since that day.

— **Jerome Murray**

I was in eighth grade. The whole school had to go to the Stations of the Cross. Sister left me and two friends back at school to do some work for her. All three of us were well behaved, good students, etc. We got the work done and then ran up and down the hall screaming. We went to the office and rang the bell again and again. We went wild! We kept this up for one-half hour. Great therapy for Catholic school kids.

— **Debbie Duffy**

Superior Catholics

I really enjoyed clapping the erasers and watering the plants, but only the boys got to open the tall windows. They used a long stick with a hook on it. The windows had thirty panels of curtains and they needed to be washed and I would always raise my hand and say my mother would do it. When I would give them to her she would smile and say, "Like I don't have enough to do." The nuns did not live near the school, but at 1614 Belknap. They could not be on the street alone so one of the children would have to stay behind and walk them home. The janitor at Sacred Heart was named Mr. Ledwidge and he was always in the furnace room putting coal in the furnace. He also let the boys come down and smoke in that room. The nuns were always collecting money for pagan babies. To ransom a baby, we had to collect $5.00. Then we got to name the baby, and we always chose the name Joseph. We also raised money to buy Father a sick call burse. It was the equipment he needed to bring sacraments to people. The eighth grade girls got to make the altar bread for the hosts. We used a very special fine flour call lillium. I remember the names of many of the nuns I had at Sacred Heart. They were: Sister Mercedes, Sister Evangeline, Sister Santina, Sister Ernesta, Sister Alicia, Sister Adella, Sister Evangela. Sister Tides taught algebra, Sister Paulinda taught ancient history. Father Owens came and taught religion and handed out report cards. He always made jokes when he did this so people would feel good about their report cards.

— **Rose Corcoran Bogan**

Cathedral

Father Green always said couches were dynamite - stay away from them. Sister Theresina. She seemed 115 years old when she taught Latin class. She was descended from the gods. Love and Jupiter were her parents. Now for the sports. We beat Senior High 9 out 10 of times when we played them in basketball.

— **Mark Frodesen**

Many Superior Cathedralites will remember Sister Henriella. She was a great science teacher and was very loyal to each student. She meant business when it came to making sure every student succeeded in her sciences classes. Sister Henriella's loyalty extended beyond the classroom. The former Cathedral Panthers football and basketball teams could always look up in the stands and see her cheering them on. Her loyalty to Cathedralites extended to each of these sports players as they graduated and moved on to Superior Senior High School. Former Cathedral graduates playing on the Superior Senior High Spartan football and basketball teams could still look up in the stands and see Sister Henriella cheering them on. It wasn't so much the game or their way of playing that she was cheering for. She was cheering and supporting each of them as successful individuals. Sister Henriella was very proud of them, where they came from and who they had become.

— **Susan Moselle Collins**

Superior Catholics

The nuns would send me to the convent to get their lunches. I took a wagon. The convent was around Belknap and John. I'd get in a game of marbles and I would be late with the lunches and they would be cold. I blame the non-Catholic kids for getting me in the game of marbles.
— **Jack "Blinky" Delcourt**

I was born in 1913. I went to Sacred Heart and Cathedral. Catholic school taught people the A-B-Cs, multiplication and <u>RESPECT</u>.

I was at an age when my voice was changing and the nun said, "Thomas, you be quiet when we're singing." She told me to do math instead. My voice must have improved because I sing in the choir at Cathedral now.

We had a very good football team. We were undefeated and <u>unscored</u> upon when I was a sophomore. I have never forgotten that. I still feel proud when I think of the great guys on the team and that time in my life.
— **Thomas Higgins**

Cathedral

Friends posing for the camera on a High Holy Day.

Claude Allouez Academy

Ora pro nobis

Claude Allouez Academy

Superior Catholics

At first, the tiny school located at 2202 John Avenue was intended to be an educational institution run by the Jesuits exclusively for boys. In 1915 the Jesuits had to abandon their plan and prevailed upon the Sisters of St. Joseph to buy the property and open it as a girls' academy. In September of 1915, St. Joseph's Academy opened its doors to an enrollment of 13 girls. Each year the number of students increased, and by 1917, a four-year high school program of classical studies was made available. The academy was the first Catholic high school for girls in Superior with its first graduate being Mary Crawford, daughter of W.P. Crawford, a local attorney. In March of 1924 fire struck the academy, destroying the original structure. The Sisters of St. Joseph were undaunted by this setback and by September of the same year had rebuilt the academy and opened it as an elementary school for boys and girls and a high school for girls. The building now contained an auditorium, reception rooms, a refrectory, sleeping rooms for the teachers and boarding students and six classrooms. Initially the Jesuits had chosen to name the school after Father Claude Allouez, a Jesuit missionary famous in the area, and the Sisters decided to retain it for their new school. High school classes continued to be offered at Claude Allouez Academy until 1946 when the students were absorbed into Cathedral High School. By 1955 the Sisters of St. Joseph were finding it difficult to staff the school. They approached Bishop Joseph Annabring about closing the academy and sending the students to Cathedral

Claude Allouez Academy

Grade School, but he prevailed upon the nuns to keep the school open for the younger children who would have a difficult time crossing the busy streets to reach Cathedral. The Sisters agreed to his plan of having them retain ownership of the building while their salaries and maintenance would be provided by the Cathedral parish. Finally, in 1964, the Claude Allouez Academy closed its doors. The Sisters of St. Joseph no longer had enough teachers to educate the neighborhood children and by 1968 the stately old building had been turned into apartments.

Superior Catholics

MEMORIES OF:
CLAUDE ALLOUEZ ACADEMY

In second grade the work was easy and I got done before a lot of other people so I loved to read encyclopedias. When the nun caught me doing this, she made me stop. That's when I really started getting in trouble.

— **Mike Duffy**

My sister and I are twins. We were in the same class, but the nuns decided to split us up. When my sister Mary got to school on Monday, they told her to go to another class - no explanation. Mary starts to cry and goes out in the hall and wants to go home. I come out and tell Mary not to go home. Sister comes out and calls Mary a spoiled brat and pushes her down the stairs and shoves her toward the new classroom. The nun from that classroom came out and was very nice to Mary and told the other nun she would take care of it from here. At the end of the year, the first nun had a breakdown and the second nun became Mary's favorite teacher (Sister Synesia).

— **Mary Jo LaValley**

Claude Allouez Academy

An unidentified photo of classroom and students at St. Stanislaus school. We could find no pics of Claude Allouez Academy. Photo compliments of Lucy Olaf.

St. Francis Xavier

tantum ergo sacramentum

Rosemarie Ruthgeerts-Birch's graduating class

Superior Catholics

In the fall of 1882, the Right Rev. Kilian Flasch, Bishop of LaCrosse, visited St. Francis Xavier parish and urged the members of the congregation to consider building a school. The parish had already taken on the burdens of a vestry and other additions to their church and was hard pressed to find the funds for yet another project. Luckily, a generous donation of $1,225 came from five individuals, all residents of St. Louis, Missouri. This spurred into action members of the congregation with the first contribution coming from Mrs. Louis Morrisette. The Bishop, who practiced what he preached, also contributed $100 to the fund.

The contract for St. Francis School was let in May of 1883 and work began immediately. The building, a frame structure, was three stories high with a mansard roof. The first and second floors were divided into classrooms with the third being occupied by the nuns from the order of the Sisters of St. Joseph, who would teach at the school for eleven years. The school, when finally finished, would cost the congregation approximately $4,000. A dedication ceremony was held by Rev. Eustace Vollmer on September 2, 1883.

As the parish grew, members of the congregation decided it was necessary to build a new church. On October 5, 1890, a meeting was held with Bishop Flasch and the parish building committee. By the end of the meeting $11,500 was pledged toward the cost of a new church which would replace the old structure located at East 3rd Street and 23rd Avenue East (later St. Adalbert's Church). The construction of this

St. Francis Xavier

new church made it necessary for the school and the Sisters' house to be moved across the street. During the summer of 1893, the school was almost doubled in size at a cost of $3,000. The upper story of this new structure was used as a parish hall for a time, but increased enrollment made it necessary to take it back for classrooms.

School opened once again on September 4, 1894 with 105 pupils enrolled under the instruction of the Sisters of Notre Dame. Before the end of the year, enrollment had risen to 255 which included students from kindergarten through the first two years of high school. The ever increasing number of pupils made it necessary to increase the teaching staff and also in the summer of 1898 to enlarge the Sisters' home.

By 1900 enrollment had reached 400 and a class in stenography had been included in the curriculum. Crowded conditions made it necessary to discontinue kindergarten classes and in June of 1917 the high school was closed. When St. Adalbert's congregation of East End opened their own school in the fall of 1917, enrollment declined to 230 pupils.

In September of 1930 a contract was let for the building of a new St. Francis Xavier School. The new building, designed by J.O. Bach and built by the firm of Flynn and Hoffman, would cost $79,000 and be able to accommodate 200 students.

The red brick school, designed in a Tudor Gothic style, was two stories high with an attached gymnasium of one story. There were nine classrooms, four on the first floor, an office, library, teachers' rest room,

Superior Catholics

and two lavatories on each floor.

The gymnasium, which was 42x65 feet, opened off the main corridor. It contained bleacher seating for about 200 and a stage. Beneath the bleachers were locker and shower rooms, chair storage and a ticket booth.

A dedication ceremony, attended by over 2,000 people, was held on March 15, 1931. Bishop Theodore H. Reverman, assisted by Superior clergy, conducted brief services in the church and then went to the school and blessed each of the rooms. Following the dedication, a banquet for 1,200 was prepared and served by the ladies of the parish in the church hall.

With an enrollment of only 106 in 1983, the decision was made to close St. Francis Xavier School. So it was, the parochial school with the longest history, closed its doors that year.

St. Francis Xavier

MEMORIES OF ST. FRANCIS XAVIER

Not many will remember when they lived in Allouez and went to St. Francis School. To start with we lived in Allouez and had to walk to Fourth Street and cross a real high bridge. It extended from 35th Avenue East to I believe it is 29th Avenue East. A real high span crossed the Nemadji River.

At the end of this bridge was a candy store that was operated by what we thought was a crabby old bachelor. We were not allowed in unless we had some money to spend.

He had a beautiful display of chocolate candy in the windows, which we usually stopped to drool over. One cold, cold morning one of the girls stuck her tongue on an iron bar that he had across the front and her tongue got stuck. He did come out with some warm water and help get the tongue unstuck.

We rarely took the street car. It was 5 cents. There were four of us in the family. It was too expensive.

Some cold days I can remember wearing two or three pairs of home made socks and mitts and a big scarf over our faces.

When we got to school we all went to Mass at 8 o'clock. On First Friday we went to communion and were served a cup of hot chocolate. Mass was held in the basement as it was too cold in the church proper. On Tuesday we had benediction which I always dreaded as the incense seems to bother me.

The school was a large wooden grey building. Next to that was the convent, and around the corner was

Superior Catholics

what we called the auditorium. It was seldom used as it was too hard to heat. Veterans Day we had a program for the vets, at different occasions we entertained our parents at Christmas and other holidays with a program.

There was always a nun available at the convent. If you had a toothache you were handed a clove to put in the cavity.

The furnace was old so more than once it malfunctioned and we would gather our books and go sit on the steps in the sun until it was fixed.

There were eight grades but the year I graduated they decided they would try for a high school, but they just tried it for the one year as they were unable to obtain nuns to go with a high school.

I remember the fourth grade. A new girl started school. She was so pretty, and she had the most beautiful lunches and we all seemed to wait for her to open her lunch. She had olives and pickles, some things we did not have in our lunches.

Now off to Cathedral High School.

Not too much that comes to mind as we worked so hard at getting our assignments in as if we turned in the assignments we were exempted from taking the finals at the end of the semester, which we worked hard for.

We of course had a real good football team, and we did go to the games.

The one thing that comes to mind is the store on the corner of Ogden Avenue. Mawsley I believe was the name. They had a bakery, and at noon they had

St. Francis Xavier

fresh raised doughnuts that were out of this world, two for a nickel.

— **Eva Hughes**

The nuns would make us dump out the ashes from the furnace behind the school. Then we would leave and not come back for the rest of the day.

— **Pete Sheridan**

I was in the sixth grade and my brother was in kindergarten and I was at the class for altar boys for learning their Latin properly and he was waiting for me with nothing to do and he had this winter hat and coat on that he wouldn't take off and it drove this nun crazy. "We're going to be here awhile, you'd better take your jacket off" and Sister put her hands on the hat and he said, "Take your hands off of me" and Sister said, "No, now you've got to get this off or you're going to be too warm" and he said, "Take your god damn hands off of me" and she couldn't believe this sweet little red head said that and she asked me where did he learn something like that and I said I don't know. The next day she asked my sister that was one grade ahead of me, "Where would he learn anything like that?" and my sister said, "Probably from Jim, he talks like that all the time."

— **Jim Palmer**

Superior Catholics

I was an altar boy for many years and I remember Father Francis turning around during Mass and chewing out Byrne and me because we had made a mistake or laughed in the course of altar boy duties. Then, when we got in school, Sister Mary Regis would take over and give it to us, too.

George Sheridan would serve with us, too. There were four of us and we would roll out the communion cloth and meet in the middle and all Mike had to do was look at me and I'd break out laughing. We could laugh silently. Catholic school kids learned to do a lot of things silently!

Mike and I learned our Latin by skiing down the hill at Blackstead's old place, yelling our Latin to one another.

I did get to be an altar boy again when I was an adult. Eileen and I went on vacation in Gordon and we drove into church. Father Meulemans was saying Mass and he didn't have an altar boy. He asked if there were any altar boys in the congregation and Eileen nudged me and I went up and said, "Father, it's been years" and he said, "Never mind Joe - don't worry about it - I'll announce that your altar boy skills are part of the new reform that is going on in the church."

— **Joe McDonald**

The boys in Catholic school got punished a lot, but I remember one time they punished a girl. They punished her and she threw an eraser at them and they took her in the coat room and hung her on a hook by

St. Francis Xavier

the back of her shirt all day. Her feet didn't touch the floor.

— Eileen McDonald

The boys had a sledding hill by the Burlington Northern tracks that was covered with ice and we would go down during lunch hour. One day the ice broke and we all got soaking wet. Sister Maria Adele made us all go into the coat room and take off our pants and tie our coats around our waists and come back to our desks. It was music appreciation class and none of us were listening. Sister called on Gus Meyers who wasn't paying attention. He stood up, said "Yes, Sister" and his coat dropped and he was standing there in his underwear.

— Rick Davern

I was in kindergarten. At lunch time the sixth graders told us the principal had a yard stick hanging on her wall and she was going to beat us with it. They even showed it to us. I waited for the beating. It never happened. Don't hang out with sixth graders.

— Matt Duffy

I had to get out of school one Friday to play hockey. I had to go to the convent four Saturdays in a row to make up for what I missed. The first Saturday my mom dropped me off. She drove away and I ran in the other direction. The next Saturday my mom delivered

Superior Catholics

me in person to Sister Felix. Sister took my arm and I did the work. Sister Felix was a great marble and football player and a person who made sure young boys did their schoolwork.

— **Terry Bishop**

St. Francis Xavier

**Are these kids happy or what?
Just look at those faces.**

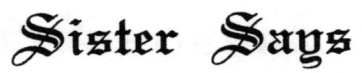

St. Louis School

In nomine patris, et filii, et spiritus sancti

Father James Gleason

Superior Catholics

A small building, next to a church which had once belonged to the Swedish Evangelical Lutheran congregation, was the first home of St. Louis School. When the doors opened on September 3, 1907, there were seventy pupils between the ages of six and fourteen years enrolled. And as these numbers increased, classes were also held in the sacristy of the church.

By 1909, the need for a new school building was evident. A special committee including Napoleon Aubin, Donat Dube, and Louis Brunette was appointed by the congregation to supervise the construction of the building. Under the direction of Father Augustine Gagnon and the committee, carpenters of the church built the two-story frame structure which was to serve the parish children until 1926.

On January 25, 1926, tragedy struck St. Louis School. Smoke was discovered pouring through the floor of the first-story landing and by the time the fire department arrived, little could be done to save the old frame structure. Fire from the overheated furnace had completely destroyed the school.

The members of the parish decided to rebuild. By the spring of 1926, plans were drawn up by the firm of R.C. Buck for a new school. The two-story brick structure, containing four classrooms and a gymnasium, was to be built on Grand Avenue between Fifth and Sixth Streets. Work began in June of 1926 and by January of 1927 the new $32,500 school was opened to the 160 students of the parish. Bishop Theodore Reverman would, in his first official func-

St. Louis School

tion as Bishop, bless the school on February 17, 1927.

Ever increasing enrollment necessitated the construction of a new $90,00 addition to the school. Groundbreaking ceremonies were held in June of 1958 for the new structure which would be located between Fourth and Fifth Streets on Grand Avenue. The new addition would house four classrooms, a principal's office and a combined health and faculty room. A public address system was also installed to serve both the new and old sections of the school. Along with the new classrooms, two more teachers would be added to the staff.

On September 7, 1966, fire once again struck St. Louis parish. This time the church building was totally consumed by flames and forced the congregation, after the fire, to conduct services in the parish hall. There was talk of building a new church and hall, but this was never to materialize.

St. Louis School served the needs of the Catholics of the North End neighborhood until June of 1974.

Superior Catholics

MEMORIES OF ST. LOUIS SCHOOL

On Friday night, after supper, we would all run down to the school and all of the children would be given lighted candles and we would walk around the church with them. I don't know why we did this, but I loved it and thought it was quite exciting. So did the other kids.

We had a great basketball team at St. Louis. I remember a kid on the team who was 6'2" in seventh grade. The North End had a lot of great athletes.

I know a lot of Catholic school kids went to schools based on their ethnic origins - St. Adalbert's was Polish, St. Anthony was Belgian, but St. Louis wasn't like that. It was a bit of everything, a real melting pot.

— Bill Schurter

Mother Ephrom, a nun from St. Louis, played poker with her students in the convent. She was a very good poker player and the losers had to pay her off in their cigarettes which she threw in the furnace.

— Sister Bonnie Alho

When I went to St. Louis it was one of the best times of my life. I went only four and a half years because I needed speech classes and St. Louis didn't have them. When my mother told me I had to go to another school, I was very upset.

St. Louis School

But my years at St. Louis were fun. I had very nice nuns for teachers.

I found out years later from a friend of mine that my third grade teacher told here I was her favorite student. That nun was Sister Agnes.

When we would go outside for recess after lunch, Father Powell would be one of the monitors. I would stand and talk to him everyday. One day we were talking and I said to him, "Father, someday you will marry me". I think I was in third grade. He said well we'll have to wait and see.

When I got married, I did ask if there was someway he could come and do it, but they said no.

When the eighth grade graduated from St. Louis (which would have been my year to graduate), they sent me a special invitation to go to graduation and dinner afterwards.

And, of course I had to sit next to Father Powell. I was nervous because we had chicken and I was sitting there wondering how to eat it. Father Powell looked at me and said, "Pick it up and eat with your fingers, that's how you eat chicken".

St. Louis School was the best experience for me and I have never forgotten it.

— **Mary Shaw Miller**

A bunch of guys and I were smoking in the back of the school during recess. Father Gleason caught us. He took us up to his office and made us smoke black rope cigarettes. All the boys got sick. I

Superior Catholics

didn't. I smoked the whole thing!

It was confirmation. The Bishop stopped at each person. We had to kiss his ring and then he would tap people on the face. He tapped me very hard and I said, "How did you find out I was a troublemaker?" My Aunt Mae (Mae Meronek) was my sponsor and she just about fainted when she heard me say that.

— Pat Shaw Anderson

For the spring concert we were suppose to be sun flowers. Our mothers had to make crepe paper costumes. We were all so excited, me included, until the nun told me I couldn't sing but only move my lips (singing talent doesn't run in our family). I was devastated and went crying to my dad who immediately wanted me out of that school. I ended up staying to finish the year, but the next year I found myself at the Ericsson School in Miss Jacubinas third grade class. My brothers and sisters followed and thus began those horrible Saturday morning Catechism classes.

I also remember a kid named Richard who for two years everyday wore gum or candy on his nose. I thought he was the dumbest thing, never learning, but now I think was was pretty smart. He was slowly driving that nun nuts.

— Barbara Carlson Meronek

I remember having to do my multiplication tables in front of the room and trying hard not to screw

St. Louis School

up. And I remember if you came late to class you had to kneel down in the doorway of the classroom and say the Lord's Prayer. That made me want to get to school on time.

— **James Norkunas**

Father Lewis was a priest at St. Louis. We called him Lulu. We would buy him cigars and he'd let us play basketball. Older people came and kicked us out. They must have bought him bigger cigars.

— **George Sheridan**

It was picture day. We were all lined up in the hall waiting for pictures to be taken. At the time, I had pretty wild hair. A "Superior Afro." The principal came down the hall. She was an old woman with a cane. She walked by me, poked me with the cane and said, "Wolf Boy doesn't get his picture taken." And I didn't.

— **David Shaw**

I had a really hard time in spelling The nuns took me to the basement of the convent after school to help me. They put me at a table and went upstairs. They forgot about me. I heard them having supper and I heard Father come over and I heard them praying. My parents didn't fine me until about 7:30 p.m. My dad was furious and he said I would be doing my work at home from then on.

— **Tim Nyberg**

St. Patrick's

Angelus domini nuntiavit Mariae

St. Patrick's school graduating class of 1941

Superior Catholics

By the 1920's, the Catholics of Billings Park had decided that it was time for them to have their own school. St. Patrick's congregation was organized in February of 1892 and had been planning for years to build a school. By the spring of 1925, their dream had become reality.

Ground was broken in May of 1925 for the new $40,000 school to be built on Lackawanna Avenue between 20th and 21st Street. It would contain four classrooms, a combination assembly hall and gymnasium, and a fully equipped kitchen. The building, which was to be two stories in height, was designed so that an additional floor could be added without disturbing the other two.

Peter B. Cadigan, local attorney, was the principal speaker at the dedication ceremonies held on September 27, 1925 to celebrate the completion of the school. He headed a program which included a violin solo of "When Irish Eyes are Smiling" by Mrs. Patrick McDonald, a violin and piano duet by Dorothy and Bernice Skeskren and a piano solo by Zora Guenard. The school opening celebration continued for a week with each night devoted to a different organization such as the Catholic Order of Foresters, the Knights of Columbus, and the Hibernians. Each group provided refreshments and entertainment for the parish.

School opened in the fall of 1925 for grades 1-7. During the first semester of 1926 the eighth grade was added. There was also talk that high school classes might be added at a later date.

In August of 1961, St. Patrick's School added two

St. Patrick's

more classrooms, a principal's office, library and conference room to its original structure. Cost the the project, which included new quarters for the Sisters, was $140,000.

By 1971, St. Patrick's School went the way of almost all the other Catholic schools in Superior and closed its doors to the children of Billings Park.

Superior Catholics

MEMORIES OF ST. PATRICK'S

It was a bitter cold day in third grade and I forgot my lunch at home. The nun I had said don't worry she would bring me one from the Mother House. I sat in the hall outside the office and waited. She finally came with a peanut butter sandwich and a green apple. I was starving. That's when I discovered she was human.

— **Lucy Turel Olaf**

For many years Sister Berchmans taught the 7th and 8th grades at St. Patrick's Grade School in Billings Park. This four room school housed two grades per classroom and often was jammed with 30 or more students. To say the least, it presented a real challenge to keep order. Sister Berchmans resorted to a "Board of Education" to help maintain control of the boys when they were roughhousing too much. This "Board" was actually a paddle (which had once been used as a toy with a long rubber band and ball attached to it). With a black marker, she had written "Sister Berchmans' Board of Education" on the back. After getting my share of cracks across the back of the hand for misbehaving in class too often, some of the other "corrected" troublemakers and I conceived a plan to "Play a Trick" on her. While she was answering the phone in the hall one day (she was also the school principal), I went up and took the "Board" and hid it and later tossed it in the old trash barrel behind the parish priest's house next to the school.

St. Patrick's

As the Saints would have it, about two or three days later, Sister Berchmans said, "The maintenance man had found it in the trash can behind St. Joe's Hospital" and had returned the paddle to her and she wanted to know "who did it". After serious questioning of the "usual suspects" (of which I was often one), wouldn't you know it, someone "squealed" on me.

Now I had nothing to do with putting that "correction tool" in the trash behind the hospital, so I thought (at the time), that I was justified in my story that, "I didn't do it."

Years later, Sister Berchmans went on to get her doctorate in education. In preparing her thesis, she interviewed a number of her students from her years as a teacher so when asked I thought it would be fun to participate. Her emphasis of questioning came to asking how discipline played a roll in teaching. I said I thought we got away with too much as it was and were not unduly treated and it was amazing we learned anything! Then we got around to the "Board of Education". So then I, "fessed-up" (after all those years), "But I only put it behind the priest's house." She said, "Well, that settles it." After all these years, one of the "other boys" (who she had just interviewed and who had been a grade ahead of me at the time of the "crime"), said he thought "I would have been sure to find it there so he confessed to moving it to the trash can in back of St. Joe's Hospital!" We laughed and agreed the "case was finally closed."

— **Dennis Drinkwine**

Superior Catholics

When I attended the eighth grade at St. Patrick's Grade School in the year of 1957, the parish had just purchased a number of new Webster dictionaries. The boys in the eighth grade had squirt gun fights whenever the Sister would leave the classroom for several minutes to take her daily 2 Bufferin tablets to help her through the rest of the day. When she returned, she observed water on the blackboard and on the floor. She would search our desks for our lethal weapons. She focused on one particular individual - Dennis Drinkwine, but she could never find the weapon for evidence. One afternoon during an exam Sister Berchmans was pacing up and down the aisles to monitor the students, when passing Dennis Drinkwine's desk her veil caught onto the dictionary that was lying on his desk and pulled it to the floor. The cover of the "new" dictionary was open and there was his squirt gun in place where he had neatly carved out the form of his gun in the pages. The good nun became so enraged she took one of the baseball bats and chased him around the classroom, connecting once. It was an unforgettable scene. Dennis was sent home from school to be reprimanded by his parents. To make matters worse for Dennis, he had two sisters that belonged to the same convent as his eighth grade teacher. Needless to say, squirt guns were never brought into the classroom after that incident.

— **Jerome Murray**

St. Patrick's

I have many stories from growing up in Billings Park and attending St. Patrick's Grade School. I am the youngest of six Murrays. In the mid fifties and early sixties, St. Patrick's had four classrooms, two grades per room. When I was in first grade, my oldest sibling, Jerry, was in eighth grade. I don't recall what I did wrong, but I was sent to the 7th and 8th grade classroom (Mother Berchmans) and had to kneel in front of my brother Jerry's row. My brother enjoyed my predicament and was making animated threats about telling our mother. While he was doing this I watched Mother Berchmans walk up from the back of the classroom. I gave him no warning whatsoever. When she reached my brother she whacked the back of his head. I was sent back to my classroom in hysterics.

I lived just across the street from St. Patrick's Church and the school was at the end of the block. The neighborhood around Lackawanna Avenue was a wonderful place to grow up. There were dozens of children on each block. We could be unruly at times, and did plenty of stupid things that kids do. But our parish priest, Father Wiegner, trusted us. At any time, we could ask for the use of the school gym. He would put the keys in his mail box. All we had to do was sweep up, turn the lights out, and return the keys when we were through.

It was a little gym with pipes that hung too low across one side of the court (only good for lay-ups, and free throws had to be shot underhanded). We loved playing basketball. There was a Murray boy on

Superior Catholics

the St. Patrick's basketball team (often two) for twelve straight years.

Being an altar boy was a big deal. The Mass was still in Latin, so it was no small feat to learn the entire mass in Latin. We served Mass a lot. We did frequent daily stretches of one to two weeks. My mother was a nurse at nearby St. Joseph's Hospital, where we often served Mass in the chapel. I remember there was the "lead" altar boy and the "other" altar boy. The lead altar boy did the fun stuff. He rang the bell at appropriate times and held the paten during communion. The other altar boy's main distinction was to switch the bible from altar to the podium prior to the sermon. It was common altar boy law that whomever arrived first was the lead altar boy. Some kids arrived before the previous Mass was finished. I hated serving with them because I rarely arrived early. But there was a way to usurp this. If you started the Mass as the lone altar boy, it was customary to begin the service and kneel in the "other" altar boy's spot. So when I had to serve with the "early birds" I would arrive a couple minutes after the Mass started and blow past him to the lead spot.

My brother Jerry was in eighth grade. He was captain of the crossing guards. When someone crossed the street illegally, you received a ticket requiring you to appear in "traffic court". Jerry, by virtue of his rank, was also the Judge. Once a week we had traffic court and violators could defend their actions. After their explanation, the Judge passed judgement and a sentence was handed down. Almost always the sen-

St. Patrick's

tence was to write a number of pages word for word out of the big Webster's Dictionary. The number of pages was relative to the offense. Jaywalking was, like...a most grievous offense. Jerry caught Mother Berchmans jaywalking during school hours. He gave her a ticket, requiring her to appear in court. Mother Berchmans reluctance to appear in court was overcome by, our then pastor, Father Corrigan. Her explanation to the Judge was not acceptable and the maximum sentence was handed out. Mother Berchmans completed the required writing.

— Tim Murray

The big mystery. What and (why) was Sister doing up in that office? How we giggled when we saw a strand of hair sticking out of that habit. Something we knew and she didn't - they couldn't look in a mirror. At 8th grade graduation the priest would give out diplomas and Sister Berchmans would wait in the wings and kiss each one as they came by.

Sister Joseph (with her arthritic fingers) gave everybody A's - God love her!

— Walter Turel

Father Breski, Polish priest of the Servite order from Chicago, they changed every two years. Tuition was $2.50 a year. "No one would be turned away if you couldn't pay," he promised my mother who was worried.

— Lucy Turel Olaf

Superior Catholics

When I was in the 4th grade at St. Patrick's School we had a spelling bee with the 8th grade students of which my brother John was in the class. We won and I was the last one standing.

St. Patrick's only had a kindergarten class for one year (1920-1931) and I was fortunate enough to be one of the students.

My sister Gertrude and I married brothers on October 5, 1946 at St. Patrick's Church with Father Breski officiating.

We used to have marble tournaments at St. Patrick's and my brother, John Herubin, was always a winner.

— **Emily Herubin Szymonowicz**

St. Patrick's School was the first in Superior to have a grade school band with Father James Gutzler.

I won an award in the school band for never having had a lesson before.

— **Robert Szymonowicz**

MEMORIES OF ST. PATRICK'S GRADE SCHOOL

The water fountain outside the large blue girls bathroom...listening and seeing a pair of black shoes/long black skirt enter the next stall. "Holy cow!!, they have to use toilets too??"

Mrs. Jodelle and long division.

The small secret room up those steps.

St. Patrick's

The fun recess periods on the wonderful swings.

Standing with folded hands waiting to pray and begin the afternoon - that is as soon as Kathy Szymonowicz would spit her gum out!

Being pulled from the classroom for a talk in the hall (never me, of course).

The smell of Sister Margaret.

MEMORIES OF ST. PATRICK'S CHURCH

The many times I had to walk out because I was feeling faint. I'd go sit atop those high steps. Sister would sometimes come out and check on me. I would always feel better being out in the cool air of Superior.

Standing in line by the big wall heaters waiting to enter the confessional. The sun streaming in the windows. Going back to the pews for a short penance.

Helping lay out the vestments just so.

Good Friday - after school and Stations of the Cross, 3 p.m., Spring had arrived. The sun would shine brilliantly, the snow had just about all melted and the water was running full force down to the sewers. A good time for a kid.

— Bernadette Olaf Larson

Second grade - I remember making a "visit" to church during lunch period. Saw a children's envelope in pew. The devil said, "Take it!". I did - there was a dime - ran to candy store - was almost

Superior Catholics

afraid to eat that candy and I confessed that sin in at least ten following confessions to make sure God heard me. What a lesson! Stayed with me for the rest of my life!

Anonymous except to God and maybe the priest!

When I was 5, my four brothers and sisters and I stayed at the St. Joseph's Childrens Home while our mom recovered from surgery. In those days recovering from surgery was a much more drawnout affair than it is today.

We were separated from one another, the boys from the girls and the younger from the older. The whole event was pretty traumatic, being separated from our parents and from each other.

The nuns who worked at the orphanage were pretty strict. We could not leave the breakfast table unless we ate our oatmeal. To this day, I hate everything about oatmeal.

One event about our stay at the orphanage is particularly memorable to me. At our home, we had a coal furnace to heat the house. We had a coal chute and a huge truck drove into the yard and dumped tons of coal right into the coal bin in the basement. One of the first things I noticed in the dorm room at the Children's Home was a door on the floor that I assumed was the coal chute. In no time at all I would discover it's real use.

One morning, the nuns who supervised our room came in, opened the doors on the floor and began shov-

St. Patrick's

ing kids into the door and down the chute. I realized immediately that the kids were being fed into the furnace to be used as fuel to keep the place warm. I was terrified. I realized my final goal in life was to find my sister so we could go to eternity together. I got behind my sister, grabbed her ponytail and held on for dear life. I remember going down the chute, fighting all the way.

The next thing I knew I was flat on my back, staring up to the sky. I wondered if it was heaven or ...?

Remember that huge tube stuck to the side of the Children's Home? As it turns out, that was the fire escape and we had just come down it. There was a man at the bottom catching kids who came out feet first, the same way they went in. I, on the other hand, had struggled and fought so hard that I turned myself around, coming out head first. I think he was so surprised that I was turned around that he just let me land. How much easier it would have been to just tell us about the drill.

I also remember the cartons of milk outside each classroom door - getting warm.

— **Rhoda Lee Nagorski**

Superior Catholics

We had a nun named Sister Berchmans and she had hay fever. We would pick dandelions at lunch time and put them in her waste basket and she would sneeze all afternoon and wouldn't teach anything. I got to crown the Blessed Virgin once and it was really an honor. It is true - we really couldn't wear patent leather shoes. There was a kid in St. Pat's named Lester Byrd and I remember a nun that said, "Lester Board go to the bird."

— Catherine Murphy

We had a nun at St. Pat's named Sister Geraldine and the kids called her Sister Jellybean. I remember Sister Cecilia went after a kid and chased him around the room and he jumped out the window, landed on the roof of the auditorium, jumped to the ground and went home. A lot of Polish people went to St. Pat's because Father H.A. Breski was the priest there and he spoke Polish. We called him Papa Breski and he would always come to our house and play cards. He was a great guy. I remember everyone marching from the church to school during Lent singing "Orapronobis" (Pray for Us). It was beautiful.

— John Murphy

St. Patrick's

Boy's CLASSES IN THE YEAR OF 1926
LEFT TO RIGHT
TOP ROW - LAWRENCE JEFFRIES - STEVE LIPPAI - ROLAND MURRAY
2ND ROW - GEORGE DRESSER - ALBERT CHEVALIER - LESTER BYRD
SISTERS BIRCHMANS ANGELITA - JOSEPH - JOHN TYLENDA - JOHN LEVINGS
COLEMAN MANNING
3RD ROW - FR HEALY - ED STACK ERWIN LEVINGS -   RUSS. McNAMAR
ALEX KOTTER - WALLY LAFLAMME - CARL GULLO - DOMINIC GULLO - LEO SICORSKI
GENE DRESSER - LEROY DRAHOTA - FR. MARMEY
4TH ROW - BEN LEVINGS - ? - JEROME FRASER - CLARENCE LAFLAMME -
CHAUNCEY BANGS - BILL SCHMIDT - E MANNING - JIM CHAPMAN - ED SCHMIDT
PHIL RAFFERTY - JIM McKPHY - JOE GALL
5TH ROW - BILL HAYNES - SAM GULLO - ARCHIE COLLINS -
FRANK CHAPMAN - ED CAMPBELL - JACK FLYNN - MANNING -
JOHN DANIELSON - ERNIE McDONNELL - EDDIE CHEVALIER - MORRIS VANH
6TH ROW - FRANK GULLO - DON LEVINGS - JOE LENIHAN -
HAROLD BANGS - PALKO - CLAYTON LAFLAMME - JACK HAASIS
JOE PAULUS - TOMMY HAYNES - TOMMY ARMSTRONG - VINCENT EGAN
EDDIE EGAN - ? - ?

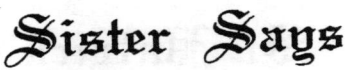
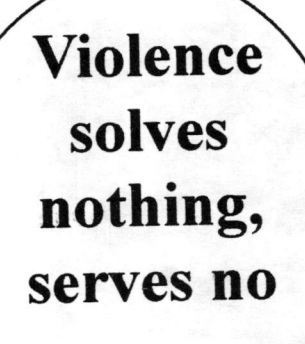

𝔖𝔱. 𝔖𝔱𝔞𝔫𝔦𝔰𝔩𝔞𝔲𝔰

Dominic go friscum

Kindergarten, 1st & 2nd grade class of 1951, St. Stanaslaus School. Photo courtesy of Lucille Olaf.

Superior Catholics

The year was 1901 and the Polish Catholics of Superior were anxious to organize their own church. Services were first held in St. Joseph's Church building, but by 1902 the congregation had obtained property on Birch Avenue and moved an unoccupied building to the site. This was the beginning of St. Stanislaus Parish.

Reverand August Babinski assumed charge of the parish in 1902 and immediately established a school on the first floor of the church building. The school opened in 1903 with one lay teacher. It was later staffed by the Sisters of the Order of St. Francis of Milwaukee and in 1909 taken over by the Sisters of St. Joseph.

By 1915 the congregation had outgrown both the church and the school. Having been well served by the combination of a church and school in one, the parish decided to build their new structure the same way. The cornerstone was laid on October 18, 1915. The blessing of the stone, which contained names of church officials, coins, copies of the daily newspapers, and the names of those giving more than fifty dollars toward the building fund, was done by Father A.A. Jazdzewski of St. Adalbert's Church.

By May of 1916 the structure was complete and ready to be dedicated. The building was 140 by 60 feet in size with a basement and three stories. The school, which would once again occupy the first floor, contained eight classrooms, an auditorium with a complete moving picture theater with seating for 400, kitchen, parlors and a gymnasium with showers that

St. Stanislaus

was open not only to the pupils but also members of the parish.

On May 21, 1916, a parade, headed by Joseph Sawicki and Ed Kolanek, was formed at Broadway Street and Tower Avenue to celebrate the completion of St. Stanislaus Church and School. Those marching in the parade included the Superior City Bank, Pulaski Guards, the Duluth Uhlans and several of the Superior and Duluth Catholic societies. Following the societies was the carriage of Bishop J.M. Koudelka with an escort of four mounted guards. The blessing of the church was followed by a High Mass sung by Father A.A. Jazdzewski and a sermon by Father Iciek of Duluth. After the services, a dinner was served by the ladies of the parish in the church parlors.

St. Stanislaus School would close its doors in 1968 and by 1982 the building would be torn down, leaving just memories of this once magnificent structure.

Superior Catholics

MEMORIES OF ST. STANISLAUS SCHOOL

As altar boys we often rated the priests. After mass Father Husnik was good for a dime. Father Nowak was good for a quarter. Monsignor Nowacki was good for no money at all. The older altar boys all got to serve for Father Nowak.

— **John Pioro**

It was a beautiful Saturday and I was serving Mass and Monsignor Nowacki asked me to go golfing "with" him after Mass. I carried his golf bag for nine holes and on the last hole he said I could hit the ball (but he did buy me a banana split at the end of the day).

— **John Pioro**

I was in a school play singing a duet with another student. When we finished, everyone was clapping so much we came back for an encore. After that they were still clapping and I thought they were making fun of me so I took off and started for home. They sent a kid after me, but it was Martha Kemp, Monsignor's housekeeper, who finally cooled me down. She was a wonderful lady and like a mother to me. She talked me into going back.

— **John Pioro**

St. Stanislaus

When I was a grown and married woman, Monsignor Nowacki would often come to the house unannounced. He would just open the door and walk in. One day my daughter, JoAnn, came home from school and found Monsignor asleep on a kitchen chair. JoAnn just let him sleep there until I got home.

— Lucy Olaf

We had a nun who loved to play football with us. One day we were playing and her veil was knocked off. I ran home and yelled to my parents, "Sister's got hair!"

— Rob Pioro

My mom proudly sat in church waiting for her son to serve Mass for the first time. She broke into a sweat when he starts lighting the high candles and can't locate the wick. I went to the eye doctor and wore glasses from that time on. Still wearing them at the age of 80.

— Stan Turel

In November of 1948 Walter Mizinski organized the Kosciuszko Ladies Auxiliary to the Men's Fraternal Aid Society. To entice enrollment he collected many gifts from Superior businesses to be used as door prizes. Successfully organized a group of about one hundred members. Rules of membership were: had to be Catholic of Polish descent or married to some-

Superior Catholics

one who was Polish. The group was active and will be celebrating their 50th anniversary soon. They still continue to meet, but only about twenty are still active. The Polish Club on Broadway (former Redman Hall) has now been sold to Norm's Beer Bar, but the group still meets there. Enrollment rules have changed dramatically.

— Lucy Turel Olaf

Tony Jenda brought his pet white rat to school to scare the girls. The nun scolded him so he hid it in the ink well. Not much learnin' that day!

— Phyllis Turel

Thanks to Sister Alberta for sparing my life. I came to class two hours late after playing at the stockyards near the Slovak church (Sts. Cyril & Methodius on Pine Avenue). It was also known as the Soo Line Church.

— Walter Turel

I had a new pair of Hi Top Boots with a built in pouch for my shiny jackknife. No problem in carrying a knife in those days.

— Stan Turel

St. Stanislaus

I walked from Billings Park to St. Stanislaus School (about two miles) even on bitterly cold days. After school we would slide on the hills and then walk home over the Belknap viaduct and wait for the steam engines under the bridge to blow steam up so we could get warm.

— **Phyllis Turel**

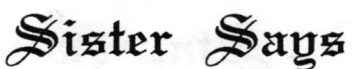

Superior Catholic Wanna-bes

The publisher's First Communion with his Godmother Ann Brozovich.

Superior Catholics

My name is Dan Vaught. I grew up north of the Twin Cities and attended grades 1 through 8 at St. Stephen's School in Anoka, Minnesota from the late 1960's through the mid 1970's. I'm honored to have an opportunity to relate one of my favorite memories of Catholic grade school. It's one that still calls me into action even now, some 30 years later. In 1966-67, I had the pleasure of being part of Sister Immaculata's first grade class. My guess is that she was in her early fifties at the time, although she could have been younger. You know how kids are when trying to determine the age of adults! Whatever her age, I clearly remember her as a gentle lady with an easy smile and a whole lot of love to give. Like all the other children, I felt the warmth of her caring attitude on a daily basis. Her love for the Lord was literally everywhere. How many of you remember writing J.M.J. at the top of your assignments? This was a daily ritual for all of us in Sister Immaculata's class no matter what subject we were working on! I guess what propels me to write about her is the unique way she taught us to extend our love and concern toward others. Two examples stand out in my mind as I reflect on this great lady. The first involves a young man Sister Immaculata knew who was overseas fighting in the Vietnam conflict. She corresponded by mail with him regularly and would read bits and pieces of the news he had to share. We became attached to this man and clearly understood that he could lose his life given the choice he made. At one point in the year, Sister offered us the opportunity to write a personal letter to

Superior Catholic Wanna-bes

our distant friend. Along with our warm wishes, she helped us put a care package together filled with candy bars, magazines, tooth brush/paste, deodorant, etc. I still remember seeing the cardboard box filled with our gifts and letters. I don't remember if it was ever received, but I hope he got it. I also hope he's alive and well today. I thought about him last February as I stood in front of the Vietnam Veterans Memorial in Washington D.C. The second way Sister Immaculata taught us to extend our love and concern to others came whenever an ambulance went by on Main Street which ran parallel to the wall of windows in our classroom. No matter what we were doing, Sister asked us to stand and together we would say a Hail Mary. It was said not only for the person in need, but also for the ambulance driver and the doctors and nurses who would care for him/her. Thirty years later, I find myself still saying a prayer when an ambulance or another emergency vehicle goes by whether I'm sitting, walking, riding or driving. I felt compelled to tell the story to my wife and children some time ago and now, we all say a Hail Mary together. As big as the world is, there is a lot of room for the positive power of prayer and well wishes directed toward those in need. It's an opportunity to connect on a spiritual level with your fellow man/woman and Lord knows we could use a bit more of that in this day and age. Rest assured that if an ambulance ever has to come for me, I know my family and Sister Immaculata will be praying for me. Her magnificent spirit and energy lives on! J.M.J.

— **Dan Vaught**

Superior Catholics

This gal stayed after school everyday (a privilege) to help Sister Aloysius wash boards and desks, windows, etc. till church bells rang 5 to 6. Sister Edwards was firm but kind. Sister Maryanda was mean. Sister Cordelia, Sup't of schools, big ruddy faced woman but so gentle. All in all I learned to respect and got a good education. Took turns being bathroom monitor - had to check so toilets weren't running, etc.

— **Florence, St. Joseph's Catholic School, Alton, Iowa**

I had very long braids in grade school. The boys would always dunk them in the inkwells we had on our desks. In 5th grade, I really had to go to the bathroom. The priest was in the room talking to the nun and I was afraid to ask to use the bathroom and I peed my pants and had to go home and change. Catholic school kids had many ways of getting out of school

— **Marcia Strand Bergquist, Marquette School, Virginia, Minnesota**

St. George's Church located on the near south side of Chicago was a mission church in that it was not self-supporting. It received the funds required to sustain it from the Archdiocese of Chicago. Almost every church in Chicago in the 1930's and 1940's and earlier, I presume, was connected with a specific nationality. Five blocks south was St. Cecilia's (Irish);

Superior Catholic Wanna-bes

six blocks southwest was St. Gabriel's (Irish) and about the same distance to the northwest was Nativity (Irish). St. George's was located in a poorer section of Chicago than its neighboring parishes and did not have the homogeneity other churches had. The school itself had eight grades, first through eight, with perhaps forty students in each grade. I attended school there from 1933 to 1941 and my classmates were the sons and daughters of parents who were immigrants from Europe. In the later 1930's many of my classmates came to school not speaking any English. They spoke German, Polish, Bohemian, Czechoslovakian and Italian; they were taught in English and acquired the language in little time. Our teachers, nuns of the Order of Saint Benedict, held classes in German for fifty cents an hour a week. Piano classes were taught on Saturday for the same price, but few families in the neighborhood could spare the money. When World War II began in September, 1939, the German classes ceased. St. George's School was very traditional in its educational program. Scholastic demands were high and standards of conduct higher. Processions were frequent with the boys wearing high, hard Eton collars with wide red satin bows in all grades and the girls with appropriate dress. Tuition was $1.00 per month which my parents could not pay. Since there were three of us children, my older brother and I spent every Saturday morning sweeping and mopping the church, followed by dusting each pew and kneeler cushions. Latin was not taught as a subject, but the boys chosen to be servers learned each response by

Superior Catholics

rote. Later I began to connect English words with Latin roots to many of the words we said as responses in the Mass and other liturgies. Six o'clock Mass in the winter was not the favorite serving assignment for any of us servers. One characteristic of Chicago Catholics is that when you were introduced to someone, you didn't ask where the person lived. You would ask what parish he or she belonged to since the assumption was that the person had to be Catholic. I believe one of my most outstanding memories occurred in sixth or seventh grade. Six or seven of us who were altar boys were running an assembly line project mailing out solicitation letters. We were instructed by the parish assistant, Father Harry, exactly what to do and how to do it. "Fold the letters in thirds across the short side." "You should remember thirds from your math class." "You put the folded letter in the envelope this way." "You lick and seal the envelope, etc." All seemed to be going well. At least we were getting out of class for a short while. However, we were brought up short when we heard Father Harry's stentorian voice bellow "Come on, George! You're doing that all bass ackwards." I think the group of us divided itself into two teams. One consisted of those who were shocked by Father Harry's knowledge of a word like that and the other grateful to Father Harry for showing us how we could say something we shouldn't and maybe - just maybe, but probably not - get away with it.

— **Thomas E. Naughton**

Superior Catholic Wanna-bes

Every Friday afternoon, during grade two, the kindly sisters ritualistically marched their charges into the church to receive the sacrament of Penance. For some mysterious reason, by the time I had reached the third grade, this practice had been abolished. It was on a Friday evening that I sat on the bed in my room, digesting my macaroni and cheese, nervously fingering my newly acquired Davey Crockett wallet, contemplating my speech. All during the week, I had been practicing my speech. My plan was to memorize it and be able to speel it off in one gigantic breath. Nervously confident, I said it half outloud, "Bless me father for I have sinned. I stole three dollars out of my mother's purse to buy myself a Davey Crockett wallet. For this and all the sins of my past life I'm sorry." That was it. I wasn't going to think about it again until I was inside the confessional. I grabbed my coat, slid into my boots, found my mittens, and searched for something to put on my head once I arrived at church. As I walked out the front door, I yelled into the kitchen that I was going to confession. The front door slammed behind me on the last syllable of confession, to avoid any questioning about my abrupt departure for confession. I had completed two blocks of the four-block walk from my house to the church. In the middle of the third block I had to pass the ice-skating rink. This was the rink that I had skated on every Friday night for the past three years, with the exception of two Friday nights when I had scarlet fever. I saw many of my classmates, noses running, cheeks pinkened, wool scarves flopping, having fun.

Superior Catholics

As I walked by, none of them noticed me. I was half hoping that one of them would look up and yell, "Hey, Mary, where are you going?" I could answer quite smugly, "Oh, I'm just going to confession." I was sure they would be astonished that I had given up an evening of skating to go to confession. After all, they'd have no way of knowing the dreadful sin I had to confess! No one gave me the opportunity to exalt myself. The church was dark except for the light around the crucifix, and the tiny crosses above the two confessionals in use. After my eyes became accustomed to the dark, I realized I wasn't alone in the church. There were two fifth graders at the communion rail, a man about my father's age waiting to go into the confessional, and a big girl in one of those shiny ski parkas two pews ahead of me. The door to the confessional on my side of the church opened and a very old lady, head penitently bent, walked out. The man, about my father's age, took the old lady's place inside the confessional. There was no Sister around to nudge me and tell me that it was my turn to stand up next to the confessional door. It was completely up to me to get up and walk over there. I looked around, thinking that perhaps there was someone in the darkness around me who had been waiting for their turn longer than I had been. My eyes shot through the darkness, searching for someone, anyone. There was no one. I thought I should run through my speech once again, just in case I'd forgotten something. "Bless me father, for I have sinned. I stole three dollars out of my mother's purse to buy myself a Davey Crockett wallet. For this

Superior Catholic Wanna-bes

and all the sins of my past life I'm sorry." As I finished the word sorry, my ears caught the sound of the confessional door swinging open. The man about the age of my father walked out. He must not have had anything big to confess, he sure wasn't in there very long. Now, the priest was in the confessional all alone, and I was kneeling outside all alone. I wondered if he would look out to see if there was anyone else waiting. I didn't ever want him to see me. He was the priest that taught us Catechism. He knew my name. I took a ragged breath, closed my eyes, opened them in time to open the door to the confessional, and knelt down inside. The priest moved the slot open and the time had come. "Bless me father, for I have sinned. I stole three dollars out of my mother's purse to buy myself a Davey Crockett wallet. For this and all the sins of my past life I'm sorry." I didn't even have time to feel relieved, for as soon as I finished my speech the priest quickly questioned me. "Did you return the money to your mother's purse?" As quickly as he asked me, I answered, "Yes." I don't recall the rest of what he said. All I could think of was that the next time I went to confession I was going to have to repeat my entire speech, plus the fact that I had lied in confession! The next thing I remember was that I was once again passing the skating rink, on my way home. As I looked over I saw the same faces laughing and screaming. Warm tears pushed their way down my cold face. I would never again be able to have that kind of fun, I had lied in confession! I walked in the front door of my house. My mom and dad had moved

Superior Catholics

from the kitchen to the living room. I said "Hi," and didn't wait to hear their response. I ran up the stairs to my bedroom and began to cry into my pillow. It seemed like about an hour had passed when my mom opened the bedroom door, sat on my bed, put her arm around me, and asked what was wrong. My automatic reply was, "Nothing." After a little motherly coaxing, I sat up and looked at her. As I looked at her, the horror of lying in confession disappeared and I felt very badly about stealing the three dollars from her purse. I had stolen money from her and here she was being nice to me. In one gigantic unrehearsed breath, I pointed to the Davey Crockett wallet on my dresser and told her that I had stolen the money to buy it out of here purse. One week later my nose was running, my cheeks were pinkened, my scarf was flapping and I was unaware of anyone walking by the skating rink on their way to confession.

— **Mary McGrath-Brooks,
Duluth, Minnesota**

One thing I remember about Catholic grade school was that several Sisters told stories about good and bad that helped me control my way of life better. One example story was an analogy about gossip. A woman had repeatedly confessed to a priest that she had told critical stories about people she knew to her friends and she was sorry for her sin and would not gossip again. Each time the priest gave her a penance of saying several prayers. Then one time after confes-

Superior Catholic Wanna-bes

sion she gossiped again, the priest said her penance was to bring a feather pillow up to the top of a hill on a windy day and to tear open the pillow to let the wind blow all the feathers out. Then she was to chase each feather and put it back in the pillow. He said this would be easier than to retrieve all of the gossip from the people she had told and from all the people they had told and from all the people they had told and from all the people they had told and from all the people they had told and from all the people they had told and from all the people they had told and from all the people they had told and from all the people they had told and from all the people they had told and from all the people they had told.

— Don Bordsen, Maplewood, Minnesota

My sister tells the story of her horrifying Easter Sunday Experience. We were members of St. Michael's in Iron River, Wisconsin. For some odd reason the Old Man wasn't on a bender that spring. The whole family had readied themselves for church. Everyone so wanted to be normal, especially my sister who always took the family situation very seriously. Ma fussed over everyone's appearance. It was difficult to make a rag-tag bunch of poor kids look presentable, but she managed minor miracles on whatever money the Old Man didn't lose at the poker table or spend on drink in the bars.

This Easter my older sister had been bequeathed a gorgeous white dress complete with patent leather

Superior Catholics

spats. The requisite hat and purse matched the dress perfectly. Her heart was aflutter for weeks in anticipation of the day when she could don the "purest, whitest, most beautifulest dress in the whole entire world."

Apparently there was an added incentive. The Old Man was actually present. For some reason, the older siblings put some stock in the drunken head of the family. Whatever.

My sister, impeccable in her duds, twirled around the shabby living room as if she were in a palace ballroom. The Old Man harumphed and got the car started. It was his job, as a proper family man, to drive the tribe to church.

Warm and beautiful that morning was. So warm in fact that sister rolled down the back window of the old Ford, the better to let in the spring air and, perhaps, let those friends of hers who were walking to church, see her framed in finery.

What sister had failed to consider was her Old Man's penchant for the chaw. A more broken hearted little girly you've never seen, I'm told, when, juiced up from his tebaccy, the Old Man let fly with a long stream of his foul expectorant. Aerodynamics being what they are, the snoose juice squirting out the front window, reentered through the back and splatted all over sister and her princess dress.

Suffice it to say, she didn't make Mass.

— **Mike Savage**

Superior Catholic Wanna-bes

Habits and Brooms

Seventh grade is a hard year anyway. Girls grow too tall for their plaid jumpers, so they graduate to green plaid skirts that hang gunnysack-like on too narrow hips. Boys are still shorter than the girls, and hope that the whispers and tightly folder notes bear no evil about them. Longing looks are cast from both sexes upon the eighth graders; would we ever reach that golden year at St. Joseph's Catholic grade school when our attitudes can hint boldly of our rank and status?

And so it was that Mrs. Blount's seventh grade class settled into a holding pattern. We were caught between not daring to look interested in anything, and intently desiring to time warp into those revered eighth graders. This required extreme self-control, reserve, and acting ability for the normal adolescent. Not only must this holding pattern permeate our general attitude; it must stay intact despite any unusual or extreme incident within everyday classroom life. The day our principal, Sister Illuminata, walked into the broom closet, our seventh grade smugness almost collapsed.

Mrs. Blount's math class was not noted for it's excitement; at best it encouraged our adolescent apathy. When Sister Illuminata marched into our math class with eyes ablaze, arm and forefinger extended, and gown and veil flowing in black and white authority behind her 4'11" frame, we sensed we would have at least a brief respite from algebra problems. The

Superior Catholics

respite wasn't so brief. There were other problems. As we scrambled to our feet to recite the obligatory "Good Morning Sister Illuminate," with the "morning" dutifully rising and lowering in pitch, we were briskly saluted back to our chairs. The following ten minutes are a bit of a blur. I remember a long litany of offenses being recited to the class...but then again, we were used to such tirades. However, this particular litany rivaled any we had ever heard in daily Mass. Mrs. Blount's class had committed a series of sins, and Sister Illuminata had had enough. Personally, I felt that these sins could have been classified in the venial category, but Sister's presence quickly bumped that assumption up into the mortal category. Her voice became higher and her forefinger became more pronounced. At least the band students in the group knew that a crescendo was occurring, a grand finale would follow shortly, and then it would be over. We braced ourselves. Sister Illuminata gave some final, benedictory words. They shot from her mouth like pulsed, precise arrows, intended to convict any remaining rebel among us. Then, with a whisk of her habit, she turned and strutted towards the door. Trouble was, there were two doors. The door on the left was the door of freedom to hallways and playgrounds. The door on the right was the broom closet. Sister Illuminata chose the door on the right.

    The class sat pregnantly still. Every eye was riveted on the hand on the broom closet door. Our seventh grade smugness played to our advantage. Though palms were sweaty and hearts were beating faster, we

Superior Catholic Wanna-bes

kept our facial demeanor the same. If Sister chose to suddenly turn and look at us, she wouldn't suspect anything out of the ordinary. The doorknob turned...the door opened...and Sister Illuminata disappeared.

It felt like hours. Time froze. Mrs. Blount became a statue. We knew the grand finale would be good, but nobody ever dreamed it could be like this.

How long did Sister Illuminata stay in the broom closet? Not long. In a blink of an eye, the flowing habit reappeared. She spoke not a word but walked straight out the other door. "Class, please turn to page 242 in your math books," Mrs. Blount intoned. Life goes on. It must be remembered though, that Mrs. Blount's seventh grade class never, ever, showed any emotions. But one day in April of 1968, in the middle of math class, a few smiles and snickers could be detected.

— Mary Lambrecht, Eau Claire, Wisconsin

I am not Catholic, but I grew up in East End surrounded by Catholics and I always wanted to be one. I drove my mother crazy with my Catholic obsessions. I would go to into my room and practice the Sign of the Cross. I was so jealous of my Catholic friends on Ash Wednesday because they got to have ashes on their foreheads all day. Mr. Griffen, a man who lived in the neighborhood, used to take care of the statues at St. Francis Church and he would have statues in the basement of his house once in awhile and I loved to go down there and just stare at them.

Superior Catholics

On Fridays, my friends Judy Luzaich and Ruth Shaul and I would go to the Windmill Restaurant on 2nd Street and I would insist that we order tuna fish pizza.

> **— Pat Sandstrom,
> wanted to be a Catholic**

I've never considered being a Superior Catholic, but public school kids have a few stories to tell, too. I was in fourth grade and my sister, Marsha, was in sixth. She was bugging me before school, so on the way I made a mud snowball (a snowball with a mud center) and threw it at her and hit her new coat. When she got to school, her teacher asked her what happened to her coat and she said her brother hit her with a snowball. I was sent to the principal's office and in the office was another kid named Kelly Covelli. The principal took us up to the attic. Before we left, Kelly took a seat cushion off a chair in the office and stuck it in his pants. The principal took out a garden hose and hit Kelly first and he laughed. The he made him take the cushion out and hit him a couple of times and then hit me. Neither one of us laughed after that.

> **— Roger Cheney, Bain Elementary School Kenosha, Wisconsin**

Superior Catholic Wanna-bes

Ominos, dominos, checkers, monopoly

**Barbara Ann Ruthgeerts-Byrne.
First Communion.
Isn't she just so precious?**

Superior Catholics

After the nuns started leaving their habits back in the convent, the authors started playing "Spot the Nun" at family gatherings. Now you can play too! Look for Sister Mary Agnes in her habit and in her street clothes. Can you spot her? Many thanks to **Pattie Kolar**, Georgeann's "non" Catholic friend from Duluth. MN. for the artistry.

Superior's Catholic Future

Ethan loves school at Cathedral! He thinks his teachers are nice. He thinks Sister Eva Jean is "really nice" because when his teacher sends him to the office with papers, Sister is always very happy. His biggest memory continues to be when he was so nervous when he had to serve Mass in 1st grade. His arms were still tired at the end of the day, because the communion tray was so heavy!

— Ethan, Age 7, Grade 1

People like Ethan represent the future for Superior Catholics.

We are proud of all our Catholic youth.

We love
HAPPY ENDINGS!!!

Superior Catholics

Photo Note

The photos used in this book were provided by private individuals from their personal collections. None of the photos displayed any copyright protection. Most had no photographer's imprint. Credit was given when an such an imprint or studio ID existed.

Latin Quiz Note

The answer to the quiz question on page 113 is, why the Catholic church has so much money. Every Mass, the priest stands up there and says, "Dominick, go frisk 'em."

Other Books Available from Savage Press

Hometown Wisconsin by Marshall J. Cook

Treasures from the Beginning of the World by Jeff Lewis

Stop in the Name of the Law by Alex O'Kash

A Hint of Frost — Essays from the Earth by Rusty King

Widow of the Waves by Bev Jamison

Appalachian Mettle by Paul Bennett

Gleanings from the Hillsides by E.M. Johnson

Keeper of the Town by Don Cameron

Thicker Than Water by Hazel Sangster

Moments Beautiful Moments Bright by Brett Bartholomaus

The Courtship of Sarah McClean by S & S Castleberry

Some Things You Never Forget by Clem Miller

*The Year of the Buffalo,
a novel of love and minor league baseball*
by Marshall J. Cook

Pathways by Mary B. Wadzinski

Beyond the Mine — The Pete Benzoni Story by Pete Benzoni

To order additional copies of

Superior Catholics

or receive a copy of the complete
Savage Press catalog,

contact us at:

**Tel: 1-800-732-3867
Voice and Fax: (715) 394-9513
e-mail: savpress@spacestar.com
Web Page**
www.cp.duluth.mn.us/~awest/savpress

Visa or MasterCard accepted.

Savage **PRESS**

Box 115, Superior, WI 54880 (715) 394-9513

We are always looking for good manuscripts—poetry, fiction, memoirs, family history, true crime and other genres. Send a synopsis and the first three chapters.